Contract or trust?

The role of compacts in local governance

Gary Craig, Marilyn Taylor, Kate Bloor, Mick Wilkinson with Alia Syed and Surya Monro

First published in Great Britain in January 2002 by

The Policy Press
34 Tyndall's Park Road
Bristol BS8 1PY
UK

Tel no +44 (0)117 954 6800
Fax no +44 (0)117 973 7308
E-mail tpp@bristol.ac.uk
www.policypress.org.uk

Published for the Joseph Rowntree Foundation by The Policy Press

ISBN 1 86134 379 5

Gary Craig is Professor of Social Justice, Department of Comparative and Applied Social Sciences, University of Hull, **Marilyn Taylor** is Professor of Social Policy, Health and Social Policy Research Centre, University of Brighton, where **Kate Bloor** and **Surya Monro** were formally research fellows, **Mick Wilkinson** is Research Officer at the Department of Comparative and Applied Social Sciences, University of Hull and **Alia Syed** is a freelance research consultant and trainer.

The **Joseph Rowntree Foundation** has supported this project as part of its programme of research and innovative development projects, which it hopes will be of value to policy makers, practitioners and service users. The facts presented and views expressed in this report are, however, those of the authors and not necessarily those of the Foundation.

Front cover: image supplied with the kind permission of Photodisc

Cover design by Qube Design Associates, Bristol
Printed in Great Britain by Hobbs the Printers Ltd, Southampton

Contents

Acknowledgements

The research team would like to acknowledge with thanks the help of all respondents to both studies reported here as well as to members of the project Advisory Group, which provided considerable support at meetings and at a mid-term seminar that was conducted with representatives of some of the case study sites and members of the Advisory Group in the midst of the Greete Fludde of York in November 2000. The team would also like to record its gratitude to Pat Keen, from the Joseph Rowntree Foundation (JRF), who provided supportive help throughout the course of all three of the compact studies referred to in this report.

The Advisory Group consisted of the following people (original organisational affiliations given):

Steven Maxwell, Scottish Council for Voluntary Organisations
Lucie Bolam and **Daniel Hurford**, Wales Local Government Association
Emmanuel Williams, Freelance researcher
Janis Miles, NHS Confederation
Kathryn McDermott, Southwark Community Care Forum
Kevin Lloyd, Department of the Environment, Transport and the Regions
Mike Palmer, Welsh Council for Voluntary Action
Jon Harris, Convention of Scottish Local Authorities
Elisabeth Pritchard, National Association of Councils for Voluntary Service
Simon Brereton, Action for Communities in Rural England
Helen Horton, Active Communities Unit, Home Office
Adam Gaines and **Paul Barasi**, National Council for Voluntary Organisations
Roger Sykes, Local Government Association
Bal Dhillon, National Council of Training and Enterprise Councils
Brian Ruddock, Community Sector Coalition
Lucy Gaster, University of Birmingham

Glossary of terms

BME   black and minority ethnic

CVS   Council for Voluntary Service

LDA   local development agency – a term
applied to all voluntary and community
sector intermediary bodies, including
Councils for Voluntary Services

LSPs   local strategic partnerships – the bodies
that are being set up as part of the
National Strategy for Neighborhood
Renewal to oversee renewal strategies, to
take responsibility for the Neighbourhood
Renewal Fund and to assist with
community strategies

VCO   voluntary and community organisation

VCS   voluntary and community sector(s)

VSF   voluntary sector forum – a vehicle for the
representation of the voluntary and
usually community sectors

Background to local compacts

The national compact

The changing nature of the relationship between the state and the voluntary and community sectors (VCS) has been a feature in the development of social welfare in many countries over recent decades (see for example, Wolfenden, 1978). (As with our earlier mapping study, we use the term 'VCS' to include service-providing, advocacy and campaigning organisations, and organisations with and without paid workers. It also includes the increasing number of organisations of service users and carers.) In the UK, as elsewhere, the move away from state provision towards a welfare market has changed the welfare mix and given voluntary and community organisations (VCOs) a greater role in service delivery. More recently, an emphasis on 'partnership' has signalled the growing importance of VCOs in both developing and implementing policy.

But studies of partnership – either in the welfare market (the 'so-called' contract culture) or in new forms of governance – have suggested that the state's new working relationships with the VCS, rather than being collaborative in the way that partnering suggests, can be very instrumental, reflecting a continued imbalance of power (Balloch and Taylor, 2001; Powell et al, 2002). In the UK, the development of a national compact between government and the VCS was seen as one important way to address this issue.

First suggested in England by a high profile Commission on the Future of the Voluntary Sector (Deakin, 1995) (and mirrored in similar discussions in other constituent countries of the UK), the idea of a national compact was adopted as a priority by the first New Labour government elected in 1997. The government's ambitions for it

seemed considerable: in 1999 Jack Straw, then Home Secretary, claimed that it would "not only usher in a new era of relations between government and the voluntary sector ... [but] ... foster a shared vision of an inclusive, compassionate and active society" (Hunter, 1999, p 18). This view was echoed by senior VCS representatives, with Stuart Etherington, Chief Executive of the National Council for Voluntary Organisations (NCVO) noting that it marked "a sea change in how this sector and the government will work together ... [and] ... the catalyst for more effective, consistent and even-handed relations" (Hunter, 1999, p 19). Even amid this euphoria, however, some critical voices raised the prospect that the coming together of mainstream actors around the compact might act to further marginalise those already at the margins of the VCS, the poor, black and minority groups, unpopular causes and groups (Hunter, 1999). Both Dahrendorf (2001) and others (see, for example, McCurry, 2001) have pointed to the differentials in power within the VCS between the 'institutional voluntary sector' and smaller, poorly resourced community groups.

Developed in negotiation with VCS representatives, the national compact was launched in the autumn of 1998. Separate compacts were announced in England, Scotland and Wales. (There is also a compact in Northern Ireland – indeed earlier developments there had acted as a catalyst for national compacts across the water. However, as the nature of local government in the province is different from that in the other three countries, we have not covered Northern Ireland in our research.)

Although there are significant differences between the three national compacts, reflecting the development of local forms of governance

(Bloor, 1999), they each provide a framework of principles which, in England, has been followed by a number of more detailed codes of practice – on funding, consultation, volunteering, community groups and, most latterly, on the relationship with black and minority ethnic (BME) voluntary organisations. In England and Wales, the development of national compacts also led to the encouragement of 'local compacts', the subject of this study. In Scotland, the term 'compact' was not generally used (although, for simplicity, we use the term here to cover all three countries). Here the idea of the compact had been preceded by the development of local voluntary sector policy statements, the production of which was encouraged during the process of local government reorganisation.

Why has the compact idea been taken up so enthusiastically across the three countries, both nationally and locally and by both the state and the VCS? And what is its significance? The answer depends on how one views the changing balance of power between the sectors. We could suggest four possible scenarios.

1. Senior partner

With the advent of the welfare state in the 1940s, Owen's (1964) landmark history of the voluntary sector suggested that voluntary organisations had become the junior partner in the welfare firm. In one contemporary scenario, therefore, the compact offers the VCS the opportunity to re-establish its position as a 'senior partner' – offering a framework for an even-handed relationship between the sectors that can play to the strengths of each. Such a scenario would take as genuine the claims by national government and indeed local government that they are seriously interested in the idea of community government.

2. Incorporation

A second scenario might view compacts as a more sinister attempt by government to incorporate the VCS (Colenutt and Cullen, 1994). Or they could be seen as a way of managing a sector that might otherwise, given its increasing policy salience, fly worryingly out of control.

Dahrendorf (2001) warns of the danger that the 'independence, which is the oxygen of charity might be stifled by the flirt with political power'.

3. Thin end of the wedge

It is equally possible to argue for a third scenario where the compact reflects a decisive shift in power towards the voluntary sector at the expense of local government. Local authorities are obliged by government to draw the VCS into partnership in a range of policy arenas (LGA, 2000; SEU, 2001). More perceptive local authorities may be insuring against a future when the position and powers of local government are much more heavily dependent on their willingness to work in partnership with the VCS and their ability to demonstrate this. This scenario might even see the compact as a defence strategy on the part of local authorities faced with increasing uncertainty about their own future role in local governance.

4. Irrelevance

A fourth, more pessimistic view might simply see the compact as a largely irrelevant piece of paper, unequal to the complex task of negotiation between diverse sectors in diverse environments.

The concerns the compact sought to address

It is clear that VCOs saw opportunities in the idea of a compact to address many concerns that had been troubling them for a long time. These had been brought sharply into focus with the arrival of the new public management agenda of the Conservative administrations (Ferlie et al, 1997). This agenda, with the associated move from grants to contracts, would, many felt, cast many VCOs as providers of services rather than as actors in the development of policy. Principal among these concerns were:

- longstanding worries about the security of long-term VCS funding, particularly where VCOs appeared to be disbarred from holding reserves to carry them over more difficult times;

- the inconsistency and delays that often accompanied budgeting negotiations – these were accentuated in those authorities affected by the recent structural reorganisation of local government, where the existence of some VCOs was put at risk and some organisations were obliged to cease operating (Craig and Manthorpe, 1999);
- the erosion of core and development funding with the move to contracts instead of grants, along with too much reliance on annual rather than rolling funding agreements.

All these features of the changing funding environment affected the stability and sustainability of VCOs. The move from grants to contracts also encouraged a market mentality in some local authorities which frustrated moves towards achievement of real partnership.

The idea of a compact also had the potential to address key concerns about the way that consultation had been practised in the past. These included: short timescales; an unwillingness in some public authorities to accept criticism from those they funded; the unequal balance of power; and a tendency for consultation to be tokenistic, with key decisions still made through informal networks to which VCOs did not have access. However, the context in which the national compacts emerged also raised new problems. Prominent among these were the proliferation of partnerships (Balloch and Taylor, 2001; Powell et al, 2002) which threatened to stretch the sector beyond its limits; the lack of resources to pay for partnership working; and the lack of investment in the VCS infrastructure that increasing government demands made necessary. Underpinning all these was a feeling that there was a lack of understanding in public authorities of the role, function and operational methods of the VCS (Gaster et al, 1999).

Changing profile of the VCS

Despite the above concerns, there can be no doubt that the profile of the VCS was rising even prior to the launch of the national compacts. VCOs have taken a much more prominent role in the British welfare mix over the past 30 years than they did during the main years of the welfare

state. The VCS income shot up in the years from 1979 to the late 1980s, flattened out for a few years and then rose again substantially as the delivery of welfare (and particularly social care and housing) was transferred away from local authorities. While some hoped that this would give the sector greater power in the welfare field, others feared that VCOs would simply be agents, performing the functions required by the state. This latter concern does not yet seem to be borne out by the evidence on the ground, although there are variations within the sector and between localities (Hems and Passey, 1998). There are anxieties, however, about whether investment in the sector will continue to reflect the costs of providing mainstream welfare or whether the sector will be expected to 'top up' increasingly constrained public sector funds.

The profile of the VCS increased again with the 1997 election of a New Labour government, committed to moving from 'a contract culture to a partnership culture'. Voluntary organisations were to be involved not only as service providers but as partners in policy making and in the search for solutions to some of the most persistent problems of social exclusion in the country. The Labour Party (1997) saw VCOs as having a key role because of their ability to identify unmet needs in a way which was not possible from within government and local government departmental boundaries. This addressed two of the major planks of the incoming New Labour government's policy, of creating 'joined-up' government and of tackling social exclusion (SEU, 1998). The increased profile this gave to the VCS was reflected in the enhanced status and size accorded by New Labour to the Active Communities Unit within the Home Office and has, some believe, given VCOs unprecedented access to government at national level, at least in certain policy areas (Craig et al, 2001). It was also underlined by the high priority given to agreeing a national compact by New Labour.

The development of local compacts

The English national compact was launched in the autumn of 1998 (Home Office, 1998), to be followed shortly by national compacts in Scotland and Wales. But it is at local level that many VCOs have most dealings with government. Any significant improvement in relationships would therefore depend on how far the increased profile of the sector would be reflected at local level and would affect relationships there. There was a clear commitment when the national compacts were launched to encourage the development of local compacts and this enthusiasm seemed again to be reflected at local level. Our preliminary mapping study (Craig et al, 1999), published shortly after the launch of the national compacts, also found widespread interest in the idea of local compacts both in local authorities and among local VCS bodies. Indeed many local authorities already had some kind of policy or agreement with their local VCS which could provide the basis for a local compact.

In Wales and Scotland, the process was further advanced than in England – in both countries, national intermediary bodies in each sector had joined forces to issue guidance on working together, following local government reorganisation in 1996, which produced more immediate concerns for the local VCS. Local government reorganisation in these two countries had been driven through, against considerable local opposition, by the previous Conservative administration. It created considerable initial difficulties for the VCS, both in terms of pressure on funding, the sheer pace and extent of change, and the apparent lack of concern among reorganising local authorities for the position of local VCOs (Craig and Manthorpe, 1999). Indeed in Scotland the cuts in funding to the VCS which local government reorganisation brought in its wake were so fierce that the UK government was obliged to make supplementary funding available to Scottish VCOs.

In 1999, constitutional reform in the UK devolved powers to a Scottish Parliament and a Welsh Assembly. When the Welsh Assembly was set up in the spring of 1999, the then First Minister required all Welsh local authorities to have a compact in place by the autumn of that year. Although the timescale was criticised as being too tight, it did, as one of our respondents argued, "help to move the process on". By September 2001 all Welsh authorities either had or were close to developing a local compact. In Scotland, where the term 'compact' had not been used so much at local level, all 32 unitary authorities had established voluntary sector policy statements. As we can see from the Scottish and Welsh experience with local government reorganisation, a slightly longer view suggests that centrally-

driven changes can – deliberately or by chance – be a catalyst for an improved settlement between public and voluntary/community sectors.

In England, without a central requirement to put some local mechanism in place, the development of local compacts has been much more uneven. But the picture is improving (as discussed later) and the Working Party on Government Relations, which was set up by the VCS to negotiate the national compact and the subsequent codes of practice, is working with the Local Government Association (LGA) to encourage the development of local compacts. A joint set of guidelines was published in 2000 to inform local negotiations (WGGRS/LGA, 2000). All the codes of practice attached to the national compact have now been published.

The picture in 2001

Local compacts being signed in 2001 mean that more than a third of England is now covered by compact arrangements. A large majority of local authorities are aware of the idea of a compact and more than a half are engaged in some form of discussion about it. More than four fifths of authorities view it as central to the development of the Best Value initiative and an even greater proportion view it as central to the community planning process now enshrined in the notion of local strategic partnerships.

Source: *Local Government Association survey* (Sykes and Clinton, 2000)

Changes in local governance

These developments have, of course, taken place against the background of major changes in the powers of local government. If the relationship between government as a whole and the VCS has changed over the past 20 years, so has the relationship in the UK between national and local government. Under the Thatcher administrations from 1979-90, local government found itself in a war of attrition, bearing the brunt of the withdrawal of the state from welfare and placed under considerable financial constraints. The tensions between local and central government eased under the Major administrations, but it was the election of the first New Labour government in 1997 that was seen by many in local government to herald a new dawn.

In reality, the initial apparent brightness of this dawn may have blinded many to the implications of New Labour's local government modernisation project. Local government might have more powers in principle, but it is having to earn them and individual local authorities are being subjected to greater levels of scrutiny. A swathe of legislation and other initiatives have been introduced to change the structure of local government, and to require new, more consultative approaches to service and policy making. Prominent among these are the 'best value' regime, which governs the commissioning and monitoring of public services, and the development of community strategies in consultation with a wide range of stakeholders. Local authorities are also increasingly expected to work in partnership with other bodies within a wide range of policy arenas. During the first years of the 1997 New Labour administration, a proliferation of partnerships was introduced to tackle a variety of policy issues. Now these are to be consolidated through the 'local strategic partnerships' (LSPs) mentioned above (SEU, 2001), which will operate at local authority level to tackle social exclusion, promote a more 'joined-up' approach to public service delivery and help with the development of community strategies. Similar measures have been introduced in Scotland and Wales.

The language of partnership is moving traditional ideas about government to a language of 'governance' (or even 'community governance' [Clarke and Stewart, 1997]). Governance would mean that local authorities would be just one partner (Balloch and Taylor, 2001; Powell et al, 2002) in determining the direction of local policies and services and the VCS would have a correspondingly stronger role, at least in principle. At the same time local authorities are being 'squeezed' from above and below. From above, the powers of regional government in England have been extended, with increasing powers given to government offices in the regions, with new regional development authorities and regional assemblies. If LSPs are to draw down significant government funds, they will have to be accredited by regional government offices. From below, policies aim to put local residents at the heart of new policies to transform the way services are delivered and to

reverse social exclusion in the most marginalised localities in the UK. The *National strategy for neighbourhood renewal* (SEU, 2001), which introduced the idea of LSPs, is also piloting models of neighbourhood management. These will devolve powers to neighbourhood level to ensure that mainstream budgets are delivered in 'joined-up' ways and to standards which both improve the quality of service to the consumer and give a better return on expenditure in terms of service standards.

These changes seem likely to have a profound effect on the relationship between local government and the VCS. Duties to consult over best value and community strategies should open up opportunities for the VCS to have a voice. The spread of partnerships over many policy areas gives VCOs the opportunity to contribute both to making and to implementing decisions. LSPs and neighbourhood management arrangements will require formal representation of VCOs in decision-making bodies. There is the potential to transform relationships between the local state and its VCS. This could create a very positive climate for change within local government. But while some in local government will see new opportunities in this policy environment, others could feel very threatened and defensive, creating a more negative climate for future relationships.

Where, then, does the idea of a local compact fit with this analysis and how is it perceived by those active in developing it at local levels? In the following chapters we draw on research in 12 case study sites to analyse central aspects of the process of local compact development as seen through the eyes of key local actors. In the final chapter, we discuss what place compacts have in the rapidly changing context of local governance.

Some of the ideas in this report were tested out in a mid-term workshop organised by the research team for local case study respondents (see Appendix A for details of the research on which this report is based) and interim *Findings*, drawing on discussions at that workshop, were published by the Joseph Rowntree Foundation in February 2001 (no 251). This report is published in conjunction with a further special *Findings* on the implications for BME organisations of local compact development.

2

Getting started

Driving forces

What brought the different parties to the negotiating table? Most of the English respondents in our study suggested that the lead given by central government through the national compact had been pivotal. It had given key actors in local VCOs both the confidence and a prototype to take to local authorities. It provided them with a legitimated agenda. The national lead also strengthened the arm of allies in the public sector. Local authority voluntary sector liaison officers used this lead within their authority to open doors which had been shut before. In Wales, where the chief government architect of the English compact – Alun Michael – had become First Secretary, a directive took the process further: all local authorities were required to develop a local compact and, as we have seen, within a compressed timetable.

But it was not just the national compact that brought public bodies to the negotiating table. As our earlier study showed, in Scotland and Wales, local government reorganisation had prompted action by the major national intermediary bodies, which had issued guidelines (SCVO/CoSLA,1995; SCVO, 1997a,b; WLGA/WCVA, 1997) to local government and local VCOs. Indeed, in two of our case study areas, the local compact – or its equivalent – preceded the launch of the national compact in the three countries and had been developed in anticipation of local government reorganisation. Local government reorganisation had also been a driving force in some English sites where the local authority had become a unitary authority in the late 1990s. In five of our case study sites, the compact also offered a positive strategic opportunity and a way of

tackling a broad agenda for new local development agencies (LDAs) – some formed as a result of reorganisation, but others formed to replace earlier bodies which had lost their relevance in the new local governance context. (The term 'local development agency' is used as a generic term to describe Councils for Voluntary Service [CVSs] and similar intermediary bodies which typically have an information, training and development role, and which act as a channel for communication between public authorities [or other bodies] and the VCS. This follows usage in the 1978 Wolfenden Report (Wolfenden, 1978) on the future of voluntary organisations.) In a few of the case study sites discussions had started – although progress had been slow – about the implications of regional government for the development of compacts.

There were other driving factors. As we have seen, the general move from a grants to a contracts culture during the 1990s had already given rise to a number of concerns on both sides around funding issues and the way the sector was perceived, and these concerns were reflected in all local areas. At the same time, the demands for partnership and consultation which were a dominant feature of New Labour central government policies required levels of understanding between the sectors which often did not exist and, in consequence, new approaches to decision-making. Funding – both from central government and Europe – was increasingly dependent on demonstrating partnership or consultation. Policies requiring the development of community strategies and the 'joined up' agenda of the *National Strategy for Neighbourhood Renewal* (SEU, 2001) have reinforced all these influences:

"It's not just because you think it's a good idea, it's an actual requirement now. You have to demonstrate that you are involving citizens and consumers in developing services and so you have to be able to point to the consultation and demonstrate good practice." (Public sector respondent)

We argued earlier that voluntary organisations saw an opportunity in the national compact to address many concerns that had been troubling them for a long time. But some of the incentives at local level were more immediate. In Scotland, in particular, cuts in funding to the VCS after local government reorganisation had been a major driving factor:

"It was hoped maybe to give a bit of comfort that, yes we know that times are hard but the commitment is there even if the cash isn't there at the moment. And when you are in a time of budget cuts, it is even more important to be clear about your joint priorities." (Public sector respondent)

Another factor across all three countries was the erosion of core and development funding with the move to contracts instead of grants, along with reliance on annual rather than rolling funding agreements, which provided little stability. The market mentality that accompanied the move from grants to contracts tended to frustrate the achievement of real partnership. One fear expressed in our research was that the voluntary sector would mimic the local authority in structures, terms and conditions to the extent that it lost its sense of independence. Another was that VCOs were seen primarily as service providers in some sites and not seen, especially by councillors, as having a role in policy consultation. This was a concern echoed by BME organisations which felt they were seen as a way local authorities could avoid dealing with difficult issues in relation to delivering services to local BME communities.

Funding concerns were not a new phenomenon. However, the proliferation of partnerships that accompanied New Labour policies was. The VCS was, in that sense at least, a victim of its own success. Policies which, on the face of it, favoured a better relationship with the VCS were stretching the sector beyond its limits, especially in a climate where there were rarely any resources to pay for partnership or the investment in the VCS infrastructure that government demands made necessary. There appeared in some instances to be a desperate need to rationalise.

Underpinning VCS concerns was a feeling that there was a lack of understanding in public authorities of the VCS. This was acknowledged by allies within local government. For those who were keen to work with the VCS, the compact was a tool to increase understanding across departments and other public authorities – too often the sector was seen as mainly concerned not only with service delivery but also within the narrow arena of health and social care provision. Some local authorities saw the introduction of a compact as an opportunity to create a less adversarial and confrontational approach and promote more 'realism' and professionalism within the sector. However, in one case study site, the possibility of developing a compact seems with hindsight to have taken organisations down a wrong turning since the key arena for sketching out the parameters of partnership working appears to be a regeneration partnership.

How compacts developed

A précis of how compacts were developing in all the case study sites is given in Appendix B and here we concentrate on the broader issues and trends involved. It was usually the VCS which initiated discussions on the compact – but in half the sites this interest coincided so closely with local authority agendas that it met with an immediate and positive response. In three sites, the compact was developed unilaterally – by the local authority in one site (the reason given was that the VCS infrastructure was very new) and the VCS in two others – and then presented to the other 'side'. In a further site the compact was developed between the health authority and associated health organisations, and the VCS. In one authority, the compact developed from a meeting between a local CVS and the regional government office. In two sites, compact negotiations grew out of a more general review of the VCS and its relationship with local government. In both, external consultants were brought in to carry out this review.

Five of the 12 case study and associated sites now have compacts or partnership agreements (the preferred term in Scotland). One has a partnership agreement but is seeking to have a compact. In four areas, discussion is stalled or uncertain and two are in relatively advanced draft forms. In three sites there is also a compact with the health authority and, in one case, with NHS trusts. In one area there is a compact now under negotiation with the Learning and Skills Council (LSC) – which replaced the Training and Enterprise Council (TEC) in April 2001 – and in one with all the major public bodies (except the LSC) and the regional government office:

"It's the determination of the voluntary sector forum that made those links as a starting point. Without them having made those links, they would probably not have happened. But they saw it as important to have this framework. So I undertook to get everyone round the table. To be honest, it was remarkably easy." (Public sector respondent)

In the majority of our sites, compacts were or are being developed through a small working group involving representatives of both parties – in one case the first draft was written by officers from both parties and then went out to consultation. Two were developed by the VCS. In one case the VCS then presented the compact to the statutory bodies and gave them five months to respond – which they did. Here there is now a compact in place across public authorities. But in the other site, the process has stalled and the feeling is that the local authority should have been involved earlier in the process. In one of the two sites where the local authority took the lead in developing a partnership agreement, there is now a feeling among key players from both parties that a compact would now be more appropriate.

A number of key factors have affected the development of the compacts and they will be considered in more detail in the next chapter.

The agenda

The nature – and content – of a local compact varied considerably from locality to locality. For some the national compact provided a valuable benchmark. In Scotland and Wales, the earlier work done by the LGAs and national intermediary bodies seemed equally influential in helping to shape local responses. But others were keen to distance themselves from national developments and wanted to reflect local priorities and the history of local relationships, rather than adopting the national compact wholesale. However, it was difficult to find the time and resources to do this properly at a local level and there was always a danger of adopting the national model as a default. Most compact development took place without specific earmarked additional resources being made available to the VCS or local public bodies, and this increased the pressure to take short cuts of this kind. Although there was considerable variation within local compacts which we reviewed, most at least contained reference to a core set of issues including funding, the separate roles and responsibilities of local public bodies and the VCS, consultation and timescales, and review and monitoring processes.

However, local compacts can be very broad, especially in their early stages. In at least one case, the need to get a compact agreed within a tight timescale (dictated in this case by the VCS) had left it in a rather basic form. The local authority officer concerned felt that the original draft that came from the VCS had 'no teeth', and that VCS participants had underestimated what statutory agencies would be willing to agree to. But VCOs found it could be difficult to develop an inclusive document which could accommodate the diversity of the sector without it simply becoming a lowest common denominator. Respondents emphasised the need for flexibility, especially in the commitments made by the VCS itself. What could be expected from larger VCS organisations could not always be expected from smaller groups; in this sense the compact process may have been useful in sensitising larger voluntary organisations to the needs of smaller voluntary and community groups. What seems to have been difficult here too was the feeling in many areas that speed was more important than the coverage of a compact, a clear example of the way in which the need to obtain a product sometimes overrode the concern with process.

A respondent in one site made a strong case for simplicity, arguing that only in this way could compacts apply to all the groups; while another argued that too much standardisation could kill innovation and action. The compact should not be another bureaucratic tool. In some sites, the initial broad statement was now being supplemented by the development of an action plan or of codes of practice – one key VCS player argued that, while it had been important to get the compact launched as quickly as possible, it was necessary now to take the time to work out the detail in a more careful way – in this site and one other, three codes of practice have now been developed in consultation with the wider VCS and statutory partners and more are to come. In other sites, however, the momentum had been lost once the compact was launched and the proposed action plans had never materialised; here, the compact remains at present largely 'a piece of paper'.

Funding was the dominant issue in at least four of the compacts but was raised in most areas as one of the most important concerns. In nearly every site, lack of consistency of funding practices across the local authority was a major issue. This was accompanied by a strong desire to see monitoring systems developed which could be proportional to the size of organisation and the money given to it – some kind of graduated system was being considered in one site.

But most of our respondents wanted to see compacts addressing a much wider agenda. Certainly, with the growing emphasis on partnerships as a way of working, other issues have indeed moved up the agenda. As the above discussion shows, there is a strong need to streamline partnership practices. Too much of a focus on funding not only limits the relevance of the compact to those departments in the local authority which provide funding, and those organisations in the VCS which receive it. It also institutionalises an unequal relationship and makes it more difficult for both parties to come to the process as equals. Indeed, strenuous efforts were made in one site to ensure that funding did not dominate – and there is no reference to funding in its general principles.

Summary

- The lead given by national compacts has been important in kickstarting local compact development; nonetheless most respondents were anxious that the national compact should not simply be reproduced at a local level, but should be developed to suit local circumstances.

- Many English local compacts began to develop during the study period; most Scottish and Welsh authorities already had some form of agreement in place before this study commenced.

- Major early concerns from the VCS were about inadequate funding; the huge demands placed on them through the growth of partnership working; and a failure of many members and officers to understand the wide scope of the VCS.

- Funding has been a central focus of local compacts, but partnership and consultation are becoming increasing significant; this broader balance may help to extend its relevance to the interests of smaller or more marginal VCOs.

3

Factors that influence compacts

The development of compacts has not occurred in a vacuum. While, in an ideal world, they might be seen as providing a framework within which all other developments can be set, the reality is that they have developed alongside – or sometimes just ahead of or behind – a wide range of policies that affect the relationship between the public and the VCS, sometimes informing these developments, sometimes informed by them and, not infrequently, sidelined by them.

The modernisation agenda

There is positive evidence from some of our case study sites that the compact has provided a framework which is informing other developments.

> "The compact has made a significant contribution to much broader changes and complements them, such as the best value reviews of grant aid and community development and issues about changing members' roles." (Public sector respondent)

There is also evidence that the modernisation agenda, like local government reorganisation before it, has helped to drive the compact through faster or more strongly than might otherwise have been the case. Parallel developments are also giving the VCS a much higher profile and access to some of the local people who have power. In several sites best value – the framework which replaced compulsory competitive tendering for shaping understandings of the cost-effectiveness of public services – has provided a boost for the compact, although only one of our sites had formally identified relationships with the VCS as an arena

for best value development work. Compact development appears to have informed the best value process and the two processes were seen by some of our respondents as 'intertwined'. For example, consultation over best value has been enhanced by lessons learnt from the process of compact development:

> "When we had the first stab at the action plan in 1999, BV [best value] was still a theory ... but I think this time we'll join it together." (VCS/public sector joint interview)

The need for consultation and user involvement within the best value process has promoted the need for a compact within local authorities and many VCOs, while supportive of best value as a framework for quality services, were aware of the potential ramifications of the process for them and the need to influence its direction.

Potentially more significant still is the introduction of LSPs, with their emphasis on the involvement of VCS partners. Coming towards the end of our research, it was clear that this initiative was raising the profile of the VCS and, through the Community Empowerment Fund (DLTR, 2001), providing independent resources that could act as a powerful incentive for compact development. Speaking of the Community Empowerment Fund and the requirement this places on the VCS to put a Community Network in place, a VCS respondent said:

> "I think the building of the Community Network will inevitably lead to the compact actually coming into place – and this time in relation to all parts of the LSP (ie including the new primary care team, the Learning

and Skills Council, colleges etc." (VCS respondent)

But while the modernisation agenda can be seen as supporting compact development, the overwhelming message from our research is that the pace of change has stretched the capacity of both parties and made it difficult for them to find the time to focus on a project which – except initially in Wales – does not have the tight deadlines required of other policy initiatives:

> "The Labour Group have tried so hard to consult with the community that they have overdone it. Instead of building on what's there and filling in the gaps, they have created so many different structures that noone knows what they are consulting on and with whom." (VCS respondent)

In some sites, the opportunities for the compact to inform wider developments have been lost, as the 'urgent' business of responding to each new central government initiative – even in some cases the LSP agenda – has crowded out the 'important' business of establishing the framework to inform the changes these initiatives require. Viewed as 'just another initiative' and a fairly abstract one at that (at least where the compact has not moved much beyond being just 'a piece of paper'), the development of a local compact could easily slip down the priority list, leaving the two sectors to approach each new initiative on a piecemeal basis. Respondents talked about 'impetus drift' as more urgent initiatives took up the attention of key players. When key players returned to the compact after several months, it was sometimes difficult to remember the point at which they had left earlier developments, or to recapture the spirit of the negotiations. As we shall see, the pressures of other developments also mean that compacts, once agreed, can be put on a back burner and are not always followed up by action plans.

There was general agreement that if VCOs were to play their full role, they needed the resources to ensure that frontline work did not suffer and to support the kind of infrastructure on which effective representation depends. There were additional resources provided in some case study sites for compact development and/or partnership, but against a background of cuts, they were very limited. In five of the case study sites, the local authority was either funding or had

seconded one or two staff to the VCS to help with partnership working or even specifically with compacts. In some other sites, they were funding LDAs – although funding was limited and in at least one case 'additional' funding was taken out of the existing grants budget, so did not represent extra investment. In some localities there was no direct funding for the LDA – funding came through the Lottery in one site or the Single Regeneration Budget in another. And yet we were told that the DA director in one case study site was participating in 49 partnership bodies, while a respondent in another case study site counted 83 partnerships overall. VCS respondents in two case study sites summed up the situation in almost the same words: "The current situation is unsustainable".

In Scotland, the Scottish Executive has now made a decision to give funding to local VCS development agencies in all local authority areas, which is already proving to be a really important step forward – one stipulation is that it should not replace local authority funding. In at least two sites in England the heads of the LDAs felt that the independent resources provided by the new Community Empowerment Fund had the potential to equip the VCS infrastructure to play a much fuller part:

> "I mean there is £400,000 coming in to the borough over the next three years to support voluntary and community sector infrastructure, and that's unheard of! That kind of money is going to make a hell of a difference locally, that will help us establish and support and develop all the networks that can relate to the Community Plan." (VCS respondent)

Better relationships were not just compromised by lack of resources. Some of the new initiatives were actually frustrating partnership and the principles that the compact aimed to promote. We noted earlier that best value had been a stimulus to compact development and that the two processes could be mutually beneficial. But in one case study site, there was a feeling that best value, defined in too narrow and controlling a way, would prejudice the achievement of a more equal balance between the sectors and that it might promote a market-based approach which would not benefit the VCS. There are a number of issues raised by the best value process which mirror issues raised through compact development – for example, the need for it not to be seen just as an end in itself nor to drift into a bureaucratic exercise, the importance of transparency and accountability in decision making, the importance of review and the focus on partnership (*Policy & Politics*, 2001; Walkley, 2001).

The move towards cabinet-style government at local level was also seen as a mixed blessing. Although there was one case study site where it had helped to transform a previously fragmented funding system, elsewhere voluntary organisations found that it was more difficult to penetrate than previous systems (a view echoed in other contemporary research on the VCS: Craig et al, 2001) and that it had affected consultation negatively.

Compact development can also find itself playing second fiddle to more high profile initiatives. In one authority, which had 'Pathfinder' status as part of the New Commitment to Regeneration programme initiated by the LGA, the compact had taken a back seat and had developed in isolation from the Pathfinder. It had been initiated by a VCS which now found itself making little progress on this front – it had, in a way, backed the wrong horse. However, the picture is now changing.

This section has focused mainly on modernisation in relation to local authorities. But compacts between health authorities and their local VCS had similar problems. Indeed the sheer weight and pace of the restructuring of the National Health Service had effectively halted progress in one site. The process of change here has been continuous, has caused considerable dislocation and instability and shows no signs of letting up:

> "Trying to get people to think outwards at a time when their own organisation and their own job is threatened is very difficult." (VCS respondent)

Local changes

There was evidence of frustration in some authorities with new central government policies, a frustration which could easily be displaced onto the VCS by councillors and officers who felt threatened by the new agenda. But the changes that disrupted compact development did not only come from central government. Changes in the

local political administration led to the stalling of the compact process in more than one area, and were often accompanied by funding cuts. In one site the LDA director acknowledged that relationships with the outgoing administration had not been easy, but:

> "Despite all the rows we were having with the Labour Group about cuts and how badly things were going, I don't think there is any question that compact discussions would have carried on if they'd stayed in power."

In this site, the change of administration came about as the result of a byelection. The new administration reviewed the VCS, and increased the level of cuts, which hit the BME sector particularly hard. It also discontinued regular meetings between councillors and the VCS.

Restructuring in authorities – whether in response to central government or local considerations – could also prejudice compact development by disrupting the key relationships which, as we shall see, have proved so crucial to the successful negotiation of compacts. In more than one site there had been several restructurings – both centrally and locally inspired. There are several examples in our research where the departure of a key person (a local authority chief executive, a lead member, an LDA director) had delayed the process, or even stalled it completely; or where restructuring was diverting energy and attention away from the compact process – one example was the restructuring of the health service mentioned earlier, where many actors were 'juggling for position and moving between organisations'. In this situation, the compact came fairly low down on personal agendas. However, there are equally a number of examples where the opposite was the case, and where a stalled process was revived by the arrival of a new player with commitment and enthusiasm.

Restructuring has implications for the sector beyond the compact negotiations, implications that are often completely overlooked. One example given was the merging of two local authority departments, which blurred traditional lines of engagement with the sector. Local government reorganisation provided plenty of other examples, changing departmental and corporate structures in a way that left many unclear about how to relate to the new local authority and having to negotiate their position almost from scratch. In some cases it also required the complete restructuring of the VCS infrastructure and meant that key relationships within the sector itself and with the local authority had to be redeveloped. In some cases new members, with traditions drawn from non-strategic authorities, had a limited understanding of the VCS.

Establishing trust

There is a paradox in compacts. On the one hand, the process of sitting down at a table and negotiating the processes of a compact relies on building a relationship of trust between the different parties. We argued in our previous report (Craig et al, 1999) and argue again here, that the process of developing compacts – and the trust and understanding it builds – is as important as the product. On the other hand, the need for a compact at all could be seen as a sign of the lack of trust between the partners and the need to have something in writing. This was certainly true of some of our case study sites: hence the tension between 'contract' and 'trust' inherent in the title of this report.

The opportunities provided by the compact – and the vigour with which they were pursued – depended on the natural history of the VCS and on the relationships existing between the sectors at the time, which varied considerably across the sites. In one site, it was "an opportunity to put frameworks around relationships which were already happening" (VCS respondent), but even here it was seen as an opportunity to redefine the relationship between members and the sector and promote a less paternalistic approach. In another it was an opportunity to spread protocols and relationships that were being developed within the arena of social care across the whole authority. Elsewhere, where relationships had been characterised by mistrust, it was an opportunity for the VCS to hold the local authority to account (and vice versa – compacts required commitments from voluntary organisations as well).

It might seem that developing successful compacts was most likely in the areas where there were greatest levels of trust. But this was not always the case. And maintaining trust through the process of negotiation was not

always easy. The move from grants to contracts could make people more wary, as could delays in the compact negotiations. As we shall see later, trust established between a limited number of key players was not always replicated on a wider front. In a number of sites, relationships of trust which had developed over time with one department – usually social care or social services departments – did not spread beyond this department.

In a few sites there was a long history of mistrust which needed to be addressed on both sides if progress was to be made. But while this has been possible in some areas, in others the mistrust continues to be apparent. Funding relationships have been critical in establishing trust or mistrust. Funding cuts do not always bring mistrust in their wake. As we have seen in our discussion of local government reorganisation, the potential breakdown of relationships was avoided in some sites, where previous relationships had been good, by the commitment to a compact or partnership agreement. Here the mistrust could sometimes be displaced onto central government, a common 'enemy'.

But in several other sites, the local authority itself had imposed funding cuts (in one case without any consultation) during the very period when the compact was being negotiated. In the case discussed earlier, where there had been an abrupt change in political administration, this led to a complete breakdown of trust; in another it undermined confidence in the compact process. In a third site, trust had been compromised by a number of factors: the council had been unilaterally reviewing strategic support to the sector; it was moving towards a commissioning agenda; and it was also carrying out a 'democratic legitimacy' review (of the VCS). These developments, taken together with the failure of the council to provide sufficient 'match' funding to Scottish Executive monies for the infrastructure, did little to inspire trust in the council.

In some sites, it was not the amount of funding that was critical but the nature of the funding relationship. While some respondents saw a move from grants to service level agreements as a positive, others felt it was difficult to establish trust in a contracting culture – some voluntary organisations felt that they were treated as a cheap option or as 'unpaid skivvies'. Others claimed to have been subjected to 'carrot dangling' by local authorities.

More generally, VCOs feel the relationship is too one-sided for them to feel at ease sitting across the table; the lack of trust is reflected in little ways:

> "We feel the need to send recorded letters so they can't deny they've received them." (VCS respondent)

In some sites, the negotiations are undermined by the unwillingness of senior council officers to accept the LDA as a valid channel for the views of the sector at large. Whether this is justified or not is an issue to which we will return in Chapter 4. Even in areas where good relationships had been forged with parts of the local authority, however, these could be undermined by the actions of others in the authority – who were not committed to, perhaps did not even know about – the compact. While a champion within the authority helps to move things on, sometimes that champion may be relatively isolated or, if an officer, may not have the support of members, many of whom are still distrustful of the motives of the VCS, seeing it as a challenge to their own authority. The stalling of the compact in some case study sites demonstrates how a change in leadership or political administration can undo years of building trust.

Parallel issues were raised about the way the VCS functions. The compact involves commitments from the VCS too and some respondents, from both sectors, acknowledged that mindsets needed to change in the VCS as well. Some public sector respondents still found the VCS confrontational in approach and while there are times when this may be entirely appropriate, there are others when this would be counterproductive, reinforcing prejudices on the statutory sector side of the negotiating table and entrenching existing cultures. The chief executive of one LDA explained:

> "The culture (among the VCS) is probably still rooted in the council being some sort of alien being, there is still that kind of blaming culture, blaming the council when things go wrong. That is a culture that we want to break down now. I am quite open in meetings when the subject needs broaching, to say that I think that we need

to do a little bit of growing up on our part as well. It is not just about chief officers securing their own empires; it is also about voluntary organisations waking up to the fact that equal partnerships mean equal responsibilities."

This, of course, also raises the question of tensions within the local VCS itself, which typically incorporates organisations adopting a wide range of approaches towards engagement with public policy making and public sector bodies.

Personalities

The need for trust made it inevitable that progress depended in many cases on the quality of the relationships forged between key players. It is clear from our research that progress in all case study sites has depended on the development of positive relationships between key players on both sides. There is no doubt also that in several areas the enthusiasm and positive relationship between the public authorities' lead officer and the lead person in the VCS had driven the process forward, while in others, where few tangible gains had been made, only the enthusiasm of a key local authority officer had kept the process in motion. In at least three areas, the compact or agreement was very much the product of a few committed people; in one, most compact documents were produced jointly by the lead officer in both sectors.

In two sites the leader of the council had previously had strong ties with the VCS and provided the all-important commitment from the top. Indeed it became very clear in our research that talking of the sectors as if they were entirely separate was misguided. There was a lot of cross-over between statutory bodies and this is increasingly the case as the partnership agenda marches forward. In one site, five key officers in the local authority had previously been involved in the local VCS development agency; in another, the new regeneration unit was recruiting directly from the VCS. Councillors were often involved in VCOs both officially and as volunteers (for example on management committees). This was not always seen as a positive, however. In one site at least, this had required a revision of the rules to create more distance and transparency and deal with accusations of patronage and favouritism.

Forging close working relationships can facilitate the development of compacts, but it has its dangers too. One is that the compact may not be sufficiently owned by the wider sector – and this is an issue we will return to later. The other, as we have already noted, is that the compact suffers when key people leave. Even in the few compacts we studied this was a common story. In one case study site the departure of a committed chief executive threatened the leadership of the process. In other case study sites, the recent departure of a key staff member in the public authority or a key player in the LDA had taken away the 'institutional memory', leaving other staff trying to pick up the pieces but feeling quite overwhelmed by developments about which they felt ill-informed. Equally, while the advent of a new key player can breathe new life into the process, experience in at least one case study site suggests that it can cause a further hiatus, while the incomer seeks to put his or her own mark on the initiative.

Finally, our evidence suggests that it is crucial to have the right people in key positions. While in most sites there was nothing but praise for key local authority players, in one or two sites progress had been limited by the fact that the key officer involved was inexperienced or uncommitted.

Summary

- The relationship between compact development and other key partnership initiatives has often not been thought out carefully enough; compacts can be sidelined, as a succession of new initiatives are picked up; compact development may also suffer simply because of partnership overload.

- Local authority restructuring (initiated locally or as a result of legislation) can sometimes make demands on the VCS to restructure itself; this often has to be done without additional resources and is disruptive to the VCS.

- Trust is a key component in the relationship between the VCS and statutory bodies; where this does not exist, it is difficult to find much confidence in the compact process.

- The role of individuals, both in public bodies and in the VCS, can be critical; enthusiastic and committed individuals can drive the process forward but their departure can undermine further progress.

4

Reach of the compacts

However important key relationships are, the compact will only work if it is owned by the wider voluntary/community and statutory sectors and if it is implemented across them. If there is widespread commitment, the departure of one or two key people should not make too much of a difference. This was a theme of our earlier report (Craig et al, 1999) and most case study sites in this study acknowledged that they still had a long way to go in this respect. Even in one of the case study sites that had progressed furthest – having agreed a compact with an implementation plan and review mechanisms – the local VCS development agency said, "We've failed at engaging people".

Most sites set up a Steering Group involving VCS and statutory sector representatives. This steering group normally reported back to wider consultation events in the VCS and to an appropriate local authority committee. Attendance varied but several sites reported that attendance from both sectors at meetings and events tended to be low. As a result the development of the compact tended to depend on one or two key people – in the case study sites that had progressed furthest, the major negotiations had tended to be between the manager of the LDA and a nominated officer in the local authority. Even where BME organisations were involved in compacts (or in other partnership working for that matter), BME respondents made the point that the arrangements for representation often did not acknowledge the diversity of local BME populations. It was difficult enough to get one seat at the table but one seat could not cover all BME interests. Additionally, as with many smaller community organisations, BME groups often felt they were unable to make a contribution:

"To involve groups, they need to be adequately resourced and without the staff and funding, we have decided not to go to meetings which are not deemed as a priority and for us the compact is not a priority – but I don't think we are missed either." (VCS respondent)

"We live and work in the local community and could provide expertise to the council and help them with their consultation with BME groups if only the council took an equal opportunities approach towards us." (VCS respondent)

The voluntary and community sectors

Most case study sites had an LDA (typically a CVS) or parallel body which covered the whole area. Only one – where five local authorities had been integrated into a single unitary authority during local government reorganisation – did not. Here there were five LDAs, whose make-up varied quite considerably. But even here, the five LDAs had come together in a coordinating body to facilitate their dealings with the new authority. Five of the LDAs in other sites were new, generally because of reorganisation and in one area this had been seen by both sides as a reason for the local authority taking the lead on compact development. In another area, the LDA – restructured after local government reorganisation – had closed, but a VCS forum provided a channel through which the sector could represent its interests. It was clear, however, that having an LDA did not necessarily mean that this could be used as a channel for representation. Three other case study sites had developed a VCS forum alongside the LDA as a channel for representation – two more were planning to establish one. A further three had specialist forums, although these did not link into the LDA in one case and in another they were thought to be ineffective.

Most sites reported that they had difficulty engaging people from the voluntary and especially the community sector:

> "A lot of the groups are not interested in the compact or its implementation and most of their time is spent providing [their particular] service. They have not got the time or enthusiasm to go to meetings and talk about policies." (VCS respondent)

The abstract principles of a compact are unlikely to be a priority for smaller groups whose main concern is survival and they are unlikely to have the time or resources to contribute without their frontline work suffering: "attending meetings is a luxury" (VCS respondent). But the demands of contracts and service level agreements left larger organisations, too, with little time to offer – and perhaps little motivation where they already enjoyed reasonably good relations with the local authority. A respondent from one such organisation with a turnover of £700,000 said:

> "I am not really interested in words and paper, and the process of discussion of the compact did not really inspire me, even though I think it is a good idea. I am more service-oriented than strategic." (VCS respondent)

It is worth pointing out that this lack of engagement was not confined to the compact, however. In one case study site, where the council had sent out questionnaires to VCOs about how to consult users in best practice reviews, the response had been very limited.

Our research suggested that there were real tensions between leadership and participation – between getting the compact through and involving a wide enough range of people. It also suggested that the time and resources needed to bridge the difference in culture between different parts of the sector was simply not available. LDAs found it hard to find the resources for the necessary outreach work:

> "However much stuff I send out to people they may not read it – it's personal contact that does it." (VCS respondent)

This made it particularly difficult to reflect the diversity of the sector. In some sites there were divisions within the sector which were difficult to bridge – sometimes born out of a history of perceived 'favouritism' in funding. Newer LDAs were developing their coverage and spread at the same time as they were negotiating the compact. Some case study sites had within them a variety of separate networks, making cooperative and strategic working difficult. Others reported divisions between large and small, service and campaigning organisations, radical and less radical groups. Two case study sites commented that, while organisations that were increasingly commercialised still saw themselves as part of the sector, most other VCOs did not see them in this way. A third case study site reported considerable resentment in the sector at larger organisations that 'parachuted in' and took little account of the organisations and networks already on the ground; a fourth case study site reported that larger organisations had their own networks and tended to make their own links.

It was not only larger organisations that went their own way. In some sites, the traditional dominance of social service and similar organisations meant that arts or environmental organisations preferred to make their own links, while most, though not all, BME organisations interviewed felt that the mainstream VCS structures could not represent their interests. None of the BME organisations interviewed felt that they had an effective infrastructure of their own, or even that resources were likely to be put into such an infrastructure.

However, there is evidence that in some case study sites and in some respects, the compacts process is having the positive effect of bringing the VCS together. In one site in particular it had helped to forge closer relationships between urban and rural groups via their respective representational bodies – the LDA and the Rural Community Council.

Excluded groups

In our research we asked how far the interests of community groups and BME groups were represented. (We did not explore the specific needs of other excluded groups and while some of the findings here will be transferable, these groups would also have their own particular concerns.) The importance of recognising the specific needs and concerns of these groups had been acknowledged in the national compact by the development of two special codes of practice for community groups and BME groups. It is clear that there was still some way to go in most of the case study sites we studied. One respondent made the important point that, without adequate targeted investment in community development, it was unlikely that smaller groups would be in a position to contribute. Another said:

"We aimed a lot more things in the compact to the groups who have money because we have more of a relationship with them – that's the anchor without which we can't fix the overall thing. Next year we'll fit in unfunded groups." (VCS/public sector joint interview)

A number of respondents, as we have already reported, acknowledged that they were ill-equipped to represent the interests of more marginalised groups and felt that there should be alternative channels open in order to maximise the opportunities for these groups to engage. Others were anxious to avoid the dangers of 'divide and rule'. One site had rejected the idea of a separate code of practice for community groups because they thought it would be divisive.

Concern about the potential marginalisation of BME organisations in particular led the research team to undertake a special supplementary investigation focusing on the perspectives solely of BME organisations in four case study sites (see Appendix A). Five of the 20 organisations interviewed during that supplementary study had heard of the national compact, but only one was aware of the national BME code of practice. Only two were involved in a local compact steering group:

"I went to the local seminar and recall it being said that the compact was the way forward and that the government was keen for community participation through the compact process. I was quite impressed and although I had reservations I put my name forward to remain involved but have heard nothing since and was proved right. All it was was a talk shop." (VCS respondent)

This interview was from a site where the compact process had stalled, but similar sentiments were expressed in some other case studies, including one where relationships between the BME sector and the LDA were reported by the LDA and other mainstream organisations, as well as larger BME organisations, to be relatively positive. Most BME organisations felt that they were not acting as a cohesive BME presence and only came together when there were cuts in funding. They were also concerned that BME groups were too embroiled in their own 'community politics'; divisions emerged, for example, when there was competition for limited funding. However, the main problem, which emerged in every interview, was the lack of capacity and resources in the BME sector:

"There is a lot of expectation from government that the BME sector will get involved. From our experience this is not the case. Only a handful of BME groups, ie those who are better resourced or better informed, will be able to take part. Although the compact provides an opportunity for participation of local communities in a meaningful way and may encourage political participation, there are not enough resources so only the larger organisations will benefit. The danger is that it may end up as a broad set of statements and may not mean anything to the BME voluntary and community sector." (VCS respondent)

Without an adequate infrastructure of their own, they felt it unlikely that they could have much impact:

"Participation of BME groups can only happen when they are networked, have an understanding of policy and have the resources to participate." (VCS respondent)

Most were cautious of the compact, and did not feel it had the legal authority or resources to have teeth. Indeed, several were wary that a compact could be used by more powerful local authorities to entrench their own agenda:

"I am not convinced that the compact will benefit my organisation or the BME sector since the LA [local authority] has already made decisions on major issues and initiatives. It is very difficult to challenge the LA because most organisations are funded by it. In my view the compact may be a means to give more work to the community and voluntary sector by the back door and introduce service level agreements and contracts which will be monitored vigorously." (VCS respondent)

In very few of the case study sites did we find any conscious efforts to involve the BME sector and it was clear that, where funding cuts had occurred, BME organisations seemed more likely to be cut than most. In the case study site where the compact had stalled completely, the BME sector had suffered particularly badly from the cuts in VCS funding. However, in one site a code of practice has been drawn up for the BME sector, while in another equal opportunities within the VCS had been written into the compact as a conscious commitment and was felt to be one of the major challenges for the sector.

Local authorities

There is no doubting the commitment of most of the liaison officers whose job it was to negotiate on behalf of the local authority. In a minority of case study sites, they were also backed up strongly by local political leaders. But it is also very clear that commitment to the compact is, in general, not yet spreading throughout the local authorities involved or engaging the commitment of departments whose connection with the VCS has in the past been limited. This means that the compact process can easily be undermined by officers and members who have no real engagement with the process. Respondents reported poor attendance at steering group and implementation group meetings and poor responses to consultation questionnaires and meetings.

Two main themes emerged from our interviews with respect to local authorities. The first was the absence of a corporate strategy. This was a particular problem in some of the new unitary authorities which had been created with an express expectation that corporate decision making would be a central feature of their mode of operation. The second was the lack of understanding of the VCS.

Several case study sites commented on the lack of 'joined-up thinking' in their authorities. In the past, relationships had been mainly with social services departments and perhaps departments responsible for regeneration or housing. Lack of contact between departments was the least of the problems – often there was 'persistent departmentalism' . Funding regimes overlapped and, as we have already seen, lack of consistency across funding and monitoring practices was a major issue for VCOs. It was certainly not a recipe for the effectiveness and efficiency which many public funders wanted to see. Voluntary sector liaison officers and others charged with compact negotiations often lacked the authority and status to make the agreement stick and few were given any extra resources to carry out their compact development and implementation work.

Many outside the main funding departments simply did not appear to understand the VCS:

"Too many statutory bodies still treat voluntary sector applications as if they have to avoid fraud – there are prejudices that need confronting." (VCS respondent)

One local authority respondent commented on the lack of response when she circulated draft documents to officers whose work involved them with the VCS. She argued that the compact should be part of induction and training programmes for all staff and that this training should be as challenging as equal opportunities training was in her authority. She emphasised the importance of commitment from the top – in her authority the chief executive and leader were signed up, as were senior managers. But this 'signing up' needs to translate into practice and respondents in a number of sites suggested that there were still too many officers who expected to be able to tell VCOs what to do.

Another common theme was the lack of serious involvement from councillors. Indeed some members were actively resistant, believing that the VCS undermined local democracy. Some questioned the representativeness of the key players in the VCS and felt they (the members) were better equipped to represent communities. Others, who felt threatened and uncertain about the modernisation agenda, could easily see the compact as yet another assault on their traditional role and power. Nonetheless, some respondents felt that the modernisation process could open up new opportunities, perhaps for a cabinet post with responsibility for the compact, or through ensuring that the new scrutiny process covered compact issues. Many local authorities embracing the local government modernisation agenda have yet to delineate clear cabinet responsibility for VCS liaison.

In three case study sites, reference was made to another compact – the tenants' compact – where more positive progress had sometimes been made:

> "In X this was written with the chief executive, the leader and tenants' representatives and it can go to the scrutiny panel. Tenants are trained to do surveys and contribute to audit." (Public sector respondent)

This comprehensive process compared favourably with the VCS compact even in this authority, where progress on the latter was relatively advanced. Although the two are different exercises, there is surely scope for learning across the two; this represented another area where there was a failure to 'join up' policies. One case study site also argued that there should be stronger links between the two types of compact.

Other public bodies

Many of the findings reported so far in this chapter echo issues raised in our earlier mapping report (Craig et al, 1999) and were reinforced in the interim *Findings* for this study, published early in 2001. However, there is one respect in which we can report undoubted progress and this is in the involvement of other public bodies. In four case study sites there is now a compact with the health authority – in two this also includes NHS trusts. Other sites are also exploring this possibility. In one case study site a compact was being negotiated with the local former TEC, while in another the agreement includes the regional government office, the local New Deal for Communities, the probation service, the police, the primary care group, the health authority, the NHS trust and the fire service. The key negotiators on the public sector side were the local authority and primary care group. In a third site, the most recent draft of the compact has been expanded to incorporate the structures of

the Pathfinder partnership. We only covered one site where two-tier government was in place. Here, most compact activity had centred on health bodies and the relevant district councils had only been marginally involved in compact development. This may have reflected the fact that little funding of the VCS was made at this level.

There have still been difficulties in engaging other public bodies. In one case study site the Learning and Skills Council, which covers a wider area, is reluctant to talk to three LDAs. And evidence across the case study sites does not suggest a widespread consensus about the best way of rolling out the compact – while one case study site had negotiated the compact across the public authorities and another wanted to combine the separate compacts that it had, a third preferred to work through individual arrangements before combining.

Summary

- In many areas, there were difficulties in engaging more than a few VCOs or local authority departments in the process of developing the compact; too often it was left to a small group of people or even to a few individuals.

- BME organisations largely felt excluded from the process of compact development: few felt that their needs were acknowledged or taken seriously and most felt that the compact would not offer additional support for them; only one of those interviewed had heard of the national code of practice for relationships with the BME sector.

- It can also be difficult to engage community or self-help organisations in the compact process, because of their limited resources and also because the significance of the compact may not be apparent to them.

- Within public bodies, there remained a lack of understanding about the width and scope of the VCS; in a period of change, members were more likely to be hostile to it.

- There is growing interest in the compact across other public bodies, such as NHS organisations; a growing number are engaged in the compact process.

5

Impact of the compacts

Evaluating compacts is not easy. It is extremely difficult to tell what achievements can be ascribed to the compact and what to the rest of the modernisation and partnership agenda, particularly as the partnership arena has become so crowded. Some of the changes that are required – changes in culture and attitudes, for example – are notoriously difficult to measure. It is also easy to dwell on the difficulties and disappointments. Nonetheless, the importance of the compact to key players has been demonstrated by the perseverance shown in a number of sites, and respondents in many of the sites felt that the compact – both the process of development and the finished product – had had a positive impact.

The most common response to our questions about what had been achieved was that the profile of the VCS in the public sector had increased significantly because of the compact. In one site, a respondent said that it had demonstrated to the health authority how much money the sector brought into health services locally. Two sites said that the VCS was 'being taken more seriously'. It was an important reference point:

"The council and other agencies are now accountable and the minute they do something that is not accountable we can print it and it goes out to 800 community groups." (VCS respondent)

A second common response was that the compact had been a catalyst for more information about the sector. Useful information had, for example, been collected about funding and consultation. One respondent commented that the process had 'created a dynamic situation' which has highlighted where relationships need clarifying or changing. The clarification of relationships between councillors and the sector was seen as a major positive outcome in another site. A health authority respondent commented:

"When we presented it at the HIP [Health Improvement Programme] we all had a set of overheads to use and one of them was about the level of input from the VS [voluntary sector] and if that went what a huge, huge gap it would leave for the services. I think it is issues like that and people being aware of what other people's funding cycles are, planning cycles, who we need to consult, a lot of it is just people are not clear on who we need to involve sometimes and that's why I think that it's a good thing."

VCOs also felt better informed about the local authority as a result of the compact development process.

In general, then, the compact process appears to have improved communication between the sectors. It has also raised the level of awareness both of how they each operate and of issues about boundaries and roles.

Thirdly, several sites said that service providers were consulting more and being involved in service reviews. One site said there was more open access to the local authority. A few said that informal joint working had increased and one said there was greater trust. Others could point to concrete improvements – improved funding arrangements or better complaints procedures:

"It has influenced policies towards the voluntary sector – changes to complaints procedures were discussed with the sector first." (VCS respondent)

In one site, the best value service plan was said to have been based on the compact.

A fourth common response was that the VCS was more confident in itself and working better together. One said that it had given the sector a new energy.

These comments provide some sense of gains made through the establishment of a compact process. And many of the gains were made before the compact was actually signed, as relationships improved between the sectors through the development process.

There is a virtuous circle between impact, communication and involvement. A number of sites argued that compacts needed a good communications strategy, echoing the points made earlier. Two case study sites had compact newsletters, and most others provided news about the compact through their regular mailings. In one site, when the LDA compiled a directory and produced a newsletter, there was a marked improvement in the response from the wider VCS.

One site suggested 'a logo to identify things with the compact'. Otherwise, respondents argued, people would not realise that things were changing as a consequence of the compact. This might help to get more people involved. However, not everyone agreed with the need for a high profile at the outset:

"We wanted to get the compact in without a big hoohah, without people knowing about it, because otherwise the council might have felt they were losing control and pulled away, so we've done it stealthily and now that it's in place we can review it and raise its profile." (VCS respondent)

Respondents in some case study sites argued that there needed to be 'quick wins' to keep the momentum. Otherwise expectations would be frustrated leading to disillusionment and a breakdown in trust. But others felt that it would be some years before the impact really showed:

"As the framework gets stronger then they start to see it's there – you have to keep reminding them. As we deliver more bits of the infrastructure, it gets clearer for people to see. When you ask people about the compact, they haven't the faintest idea what you are talking about. It's only when it becomes part of the structures." (Public sector respondent)

One respondent argued that a proper complaints procedure was essential if things were to change:

"Nothing will change until voluntary organisations use the compact to make complaints where its principles are not followed – things might get worse before they get better." (Public sector respondent)

There was a strong feeling that the balance of power still lay with the local authority and some of us have argued elsewhere (Craig and Taylor, 2001) that the issue of power relations is a critical one in thinking about any form of partnership working. We have already seen that in some case study sites, funding cuts were introduced without consultation at the same time as compact negotiations were going on; respondents in a number of case study sites also claimed that the sector was still not consulted on community planning and similar key initiatives, echoing this view:

"It's also about an attitudinal shift from the perception of the LA as controlling the voluntary sector to the voluntary sector being seen as an equal partner except for funding and having a range of other partnerships." (VCS respondent)

It would be fair to say that many from the VCS felt that there was a long way to go before that could be achieved. Indeed one councillor said of his authority:

"Even though they take pride that they have good relationships, people do hang onto their ideas and distrust other partners." (Public sector respondent)

A VCS respondent in another case study site observed that "the notion of equal partners is unrealistic" and felt that the local authority was using the compact as a way of keeping on top of – ie controlling – the modernisation and community governance agenda. In a third case study site, where compact negotiations were underway, VCS respondents claimed that the council appeared 'to snub the CVS at will'. In a fourth site, a VCS respondent argued that the funding relationship meant that VCOs "will never be able to argue from a position of strength". Many felt that local authorities still saw them simply as service deliverers rather than as partners in policy development. This stance was reflected in the fact that key strategic partnerships in two case study sites failed to include the VCS to any significant extent. In another case study site, VCS respondents to our study declined our invitation to a mid-term workshop to discuss the study's interim findings in case 'sharing [their] thoughts about local progress' would be construed as prejudicing their relationship with the local authority.

Fears that local authorities might use the compact to co-opt the sector were not always justified, however. In one site, the chief officer of the Voluntary Sector Forum (VSF) felt the compact could be used to counter any future threats to autonomy. Several respondents felt there had been a culture change at least in parts of the public sector. Indeed, it was two councillors – in different case study sites – who argued that the compact should underpin the independence of the sector:

> "We need to question where the voluntary sector is going – it should not just be an arm of the local authority because as such an arm it might be difficult to define what their role in decision making should be." (Public sector respondent)

> "Lobbying is still a significant role for [VCOs], even in partnership working. This independence needs to be preserved and not exploited – at times the voluntary sector has been used as a cheaper and easier option." (Public sector respondent)

However, it was clear that this view was not universally shared.

We reported earlier that the process of developing compacts had been slower than expected. Nonetheless there is a sense, at the end of this study, in some of our 'slower' case study sites that things are once again on the move. This is reinforced by information collected by the LGA and NCVO referred to earlier. A significant factor in this has been the substantial injections of resources being made available for VCS

infrastructures by the Scottish Executive and the prospect of independent resources in England through the Community Empowerment Fund. But it may also be a function of the time taken to get through the 'forming, storming and norming' process referred to in one of the sites.

Implementation and review

In Chapter 4 we commented that, if the compact is to have an impact, it will need to move beyond broad principles to implementable joint objectives:

> "The compact document is almost irrelevant, the action plan for me is what has been missing from other documents I have read. I have read an awful lot of compacts where it's just been a definition of the relationship and I thought if it was ever going to make any difference in this area it needed to be more specific." (VCS respondent)

But one of the reasons that it is, as yet, difficult for us to point to concrete changes is that implementation plans and mechanisms for review are still some way down the line in many areas. There are compacts or agreements in seven of our case study sites – both the two Scottish and Welsh case study sites, and three of the English sites. Reviews have taken place in two sites and in another, LDAs are devising their own action plans and review procedures. In yet another, review is an ongoing process through regular meetings between the VCS and its partners.

Elsewhere the situation is less satisfactory. In one Welsh authority, the implementation group is just being formed and reviews and complaints procedures will take time to develop, as indeed they will in case study sites which are still developing their compacts. In the two Scottish case study sites, intended action plans have not yet materialised and in one of these the planned monitoring group has lost considerable impetus. However, there is now a new joint working group in this case study site with plans to turn the partnership agreement into a compact. The increasing importance of the Community Planning agenda and Scottish Executive funding for the VCS infrastructure seems to have breathed new life into the process.

Implementation and review has encountered many of the problems that featured in the development process. The pace of overall change in local governance remains high and there are many other pressures on the key players. The key aspects of implementation and review have therefore taken longer than intended and attendance at implementation group meetings has been disappointing. In one case study site it was also argued that, as the process became more visible, with documents and agreements, so it became more bureaucratic and that this could slow things down. In another case study site, the fact that review meetings were delayed was making the momentum difficult to maintain. The relationships that needed to be built were not being built fast enough – representatives of the two sectors were still wary of one another. In this case study site, respondents were considering a process to reaffirm the principles of the compact, but with better communication and awareness-raising than before. Some of our respondents suggested that review should be tied into the overall local authority scrutiny process.

In one case study site where a review had been held, attendance at the review event was disappointing, but useful feedback seems still to have come out of the process. In this case study site, some of the planned tasks (like the production of a consultation map) were not carried out because the relevant officer left. Other issues raised were the need to reflect the diversity of the sector more effectively and to implement the commitments on equal opportunities. In this and other sites the importance of regular feedback to the sector and a communications strategy was stressed, as we discussed earlier in this chapter.

External scrutiny helps to drive the process. In one case study site in Wales, where the priority placed on compacts by the Welsh Assembly has given it a high profile, a respondent commented that the local authority had gained in reputation as a result of its progress on the compact. In another case study site, a respondent felt that the study on which this report is based had itself been useful in increasing the profile of the compact. A third respondent stressed the role that regional offices of central government now have in accrediting LSPs. The external scrutiny they provided gave the VCS a new kind of leverage, and a 'court of appeal'.

A number of sites wanted more information about what was happening in the development of local compacts elsewhere in the country. They felt such information was very thin on the ground. One respondent from the health service would have liked more guidance from the NHS Executive. This respondent would have liked to see the NHS Confederation promoting the compact in the same way that the LGA and its equivalents in Scotland and Wales have done in the local government arena.

Summary

- In most case study sites, respondents were able to point to gains which had been made as a result of the development of work around the compact.

- However, in the majority of areas, the issue of unequal power relations between the sectors has yet effectively to be addressed.

- The process of implementation and review is critical in maintaining momentum and this needs to be underpinned by a good communications strategy.

The future of local compacts

This study cannot provide definitive answers as to the place that local compacts may have within the arena of local governance. This is partly because an examination of the development of local compacts is an examination of work in progress, both in relation to compacts themselves but also because of the rapidly moving local government modernisation agenda. As we noted in our interim *Findings* (JRF, 2001), the policy environment at a local level is crowded and increasingly so. Early initiatives such as compacts may be displaced by newer initiatives such as LSPs or Social Inclusion Partnerships (in Scotland), especially since LSPs, for example, come with significant resources both for the partnership and community involvement. In England, both Community Chests and the Community Empowerment Fund are likely to increase the capacity of local community groups to influence policy at a local level.

Nonetheless, these newer initiatives do not make compacts irrelevant. The fact that compacts were early into the field in the developing arena of partnership working means that their influence could be considerable – if perhaps implicit – on the development of succeeding initiatives. The rapidly changing policy environment certainly raises questions about how the compact 'fits' with other initiatives but there are signs that it has an important part to play. As one respondent to an LGA survey said of best value:

"The demands of best value have made the compact all the more important in ensuring that the voluntary sector, representing a wide range of service users, can contribute to reviews. The development of more structured relationships with the voluntary sector will enable them to assist with developing innovative approaches to service delivery…."

However, as we noted earlier, the sheer pace and extent of change could mean that these opportunities for the compact experience to provide a framework for these developments could be lost as more high profile initiatives with tight deadlines take centre stage.

This is not a report about best practice, although some of our case study sites have made good progress. The intention of the study was rather to reflect the range of experience in developing compacts, so that we could draw out lessons both from what was working and what was not. We were able, by choosing a reasonably representative spread of case study sites, to reflect experience in localities with significantly different traditions and at various points in the compact development process. In some the VCS was well-established and well-funded, in others far less so; in some study sites relationships were fairly robust, in others they were marked by mistrust and suspicion; in some areas, there was a considerable degree of continuing enthusiasm to ensure that the idea of a compact took root and informed other partnership working but conversely there were some where the compact idea has barely achieved any prominence at all. What this tells us, as we argued in our earlier report (Craig et al, 1999), is that the development of a local compact needs above all to take into account local conditions and experience, local practice and resources.

One of the earlier working papers produced in the course of this study identified the key differences between the national compacts in England, Scotland and Wales (Bloor, 1999). These different frameworks reflect different policy contexts and led to a situation where, as we have seen, the development of local compacts or agreements advanced more quickly in Scotland

and Wales than in England. However, given that the overall objective of local agreements – to establish a framework of principles guiding the relationship between VCS and local public bodies – is the same within each of these three countries, it is, we believe, more helpful to focus on the key issues which are common across the three countries rather than on the different policy contexts. If compacts do continue to develop, it is reasonable to assume that developments in England will steadily catch up on those

elsewhere. One obvious learning point, however, is that it would be useful for mechanisms to be in place which would ensure that best practice in each country can be shared with other UK constituent countries so that 'the best can guide the rest'. One interesting side effect from our own study was the use of the Advisory Group as a forum for exchanging information between representatives from different countries, but it is not clear that more structured opportunities exist for this to happen.

At local level

Local compacts can provide a generic framework and guiding principles within which other partnerships can develop. If this is to happen:

- *Adequate time and resources need to be devoted to development and review:* This means dedicated officer support in both sectors and adequate resourcing for the VCS infrastructure. Additional national resources to support the infrastructure should not be at the expense of local investment.

- *The focus needs to be broader than funding issues:* A focus on funding can reinforce inequalities between the sector. A broader focus will ensure its relevance to the whole of the VCS and acknowledge the resources the VCS brings to the relationship as well as those of public bodies.

- *More attention needs to be given to ways of involving a broad range of personnel and agencies in both sectors:* Key personnel in both sectors act as champions. If they leave or if local structures or policies change significantly, compacts are vulnerable. Adequate resourcing of the VCS infrastructure will help to ensure continuity in that sector; building compact issues into induction, training, supervision and organisational development will help to spread awareness in the public sector and to ensure that the compact process can survive the departure of champions.

- *A lead from the top is essential:* Liaison officers responsible for compact development need to know that their commitments will be shared across the authority. Local authorities should consider having a Cabinet member with the VCS portfolio and building relationships with the sector into the scrutiny process.

- *Any major changes in local authority structures and procedures should take into account their likely impact on the VCS.*

- *A clear timetable and framework for review is essential* if the compact is to be more than a piece of paper.

At national level

The national lead has been critical to the development of local compacts and the resources made available to the VCS infrastructure through the Scottish Executive and the Neighbourhood Renewal strategy has the potential to breathe new life into the process. National and regional government has a continuing role to play in:

- ensuring a close 'fit' between compacts and other nationally-driven local partnership developments;

- encouraging local public sector agencies other than local and health authorities to become fully involved;

- ensuring that all local government departments 'sign up' to compact development;

- using best value and LSP frameworks to promote local compact development.

National intermediary bodies in both sectors have also played a crucial role and can help to encourage links to be made between the compact and other national policy initiatives. They can also:

- provide training and support for councillors;

- provide guidance for all local authority departments (not just those most closely involved in developing compacts) and other public sector agencies;

- establish mechanisms for the transfer of best practice within and between countries;

- pay particular attention to supporting the BME VCS and other excluded groups within compact development.

The main lessons

In our mid-term interim *Findings*, (JRF, 2001), we identified a number of key lessos from the first stages of our study. These have been reinforced by later stages of the research and lead to the following recommendations.

To elaborate on these, our study suggests that there is a particular need to pay attention to issues of: time; fit with other initiatives; trust; the need for champions; resources; the need to represent diversity; and review.

First of all, the whole process takes *time*. The development of local compacts in a number of sites was much slower than we had anticipated. This study started in 1999 with ten case study sites. In two a compact or agreement was in place; one more followed in 1999. But in all, discussion about compacts was underway. Two years later and with the added experience of two further case study sites, there are still only seven sites where compacts or partnership agreements are firmly in place. One further site is close to a fully signed up version, but in four areas – all English – progress is still uncertain or has completely stalled, while in both the Scottish sites, there is talk of translating the partnership

agreement into a compact. In half the sites, therefore, there is still some way to go. The time compact development requires will clearly depend on local circumstances, and it would be pointless to suggest an 'ideal' timetable. Much will also depend on whether the partners decide to go for speed or detail. Speed allows for a clear commitment to be signed, and has provided a firm foundation for further work in some sites. But the experience of others suggests that time may be better spent building trust between participants within the two sectors before pen is ever put to paper. Where there is a legacy of mistrust or lack of contact between the sectors, the construction of a compact is likely to be more meaningful if this development work is done first of all. Participants need to focus not only on the outcome of the exercise – the production of the 'piece of paper' – but also on the process. Indeed, a number of our respondents acknowledged that improvements in the relationship came from the process itself and preceded the actual 'piece of paper'. Developing new and more equal forms of engagement between the VCS and local public bodies is itself a gain and this should be acknowledged as such.

How compacts *fit* within the development of future partnership work remains an unanswered question at present but respondents could see a number of possibilities. One suggested that government regional offices might look for the existence of local compacts in their accreditation of LSPs, ie – that they could be used as a lever or performance indicator by which to gauge local governance relationships. However, it would be important to be clear about the reasons why a compact had not been developed in other localities. Other respondents felt that the compact could be seen as an explicit testing ground or framework for partnership working and that in future such working might learn and move on from compacts. One respondent saw it in fairly subtle terms, as establishing a way of working together:

"The only way the compact brings that additionality is by all the partnerships understanding their relationships with the voluntary sector in terms of the compact. Otherwise it just becomes one more thing to do." (VCS respondent)

In another area the compact was, a public sector respondent asserted: "A useful template for partnerships, irrespective of who the partners are".

The issue of *trust* is particularly critical in some areas, perhaps particularly in relation to councillors. In most sites, our study reveals a low level of involvement or indeed of interest among members in the compact idea. Where there was involvement, it tended as often as not to be hostile, with councillors anxious about the undermining of their own roles as democratic representatives (fears which are perhaps enhanced by the uncertainties generated by the modernisation agenda of central government). VCS members need to spend time working with key members to confront this fear.

The anxiety of councillors is ironic since there is little doubt that in terms of power, the local authority and other public bodies tend to have most of the cards stacked in their favour. Many VCOs are dependent on local public bodies, particularly local authorities, for their funding and this can leave them feeling unable to be critical. This is another aspect of the trust relationship; VCOs need to trust that punitive action – such as withdrawing funding – is not taken against organisations which choose to be critical. Unfortunately this still cannot be guaranteed in many areas. The compact needs to be a

reflection of government's assertion that local VCOs should be free 'to challenge, campaign and criticise'. The alternative is that, as some respondents feared, the compact might lead to a docile VCS thoroughly incorporated into the local authority's perspective on policy and service issues. Conversely, however, local authorities need to be reassured that criticisms made by the VCS have a firm evidential basis.

The importance of **champions** has been referred to several times in the course of this report. Clearly VCS representatives need to identify champions (who might of course be local councillors and preferably, within Cabinet local government, a councillor with a VCS portfolio). Such champions can play a number of roles. One might be to continually 'beat the drum' on behalf of the VCS. Another might be to educate other councillors and the authority as a whole as to the nature of the VCS and to encourage the collection of more information about its extent and the nature of cross-boundary relationships. Part of the educational role that champions could have would be to remind critics of the substantial contribution which the VCS makes to the local economy, providing significant added value above and beyond funding provided through central and local government (Humberside TEC, 2000; NYFVO, 2000). A third role might be to ensure that the interests of the VCS are clearly placed on the table when local authorities, as they seem to do with increasing frequency, go through major structural changes. Too often, these changes happen without proper consultation with the VCS (even where a compact is in place) and VCOs are left to catch up later on. At its best, the compact should be an explicit reminder that such structural changes affect other partners. It should ensure that they are not put into place without adequate engagement with those partners as to their impact on them.

The issue of **resources** was raised by respondents in many ways. First, the generally inadequate level of funding for the VCS in general but for the development of compact work specifically was raised many times in the course of this study. Local authorities were accused of not understanding the importance of an effective VCS infrastructure if the sector was to engage effectively and on an equal basis in the compact process and, of course, in other partnership working. In parallel, BME organisations were critical both of local authorities and of the mainstream VCS for not acknowledging the need for effective BME infrastructures, to enable them to respond to the compact process as representatives of a distinct and diverse set of interests.

As noted earlier, many respondents were concerned that local authority funding should not be used as an implicit – or in some cases explicit – lever to control the activities of the VCS. Some VCS respondents raised the possibility of independent funding for local VCS development, a prospect which is approaching reality both in Scotland and, in England, through the Community Empowerment Fund. Of course, many local VCOs do obtain funding independent of the local authority (hence the notion of added value referred to above) but this is generally short-term and small scale compared with core funding and would not offer sustainable support for local organisations. Most respondents took the view though that any independent funding should be additional to and not a replacement for local authority funding.

Despite all these issues, many respondents were keen that compact discussion should not be dominated by funding issues. Too much of a focus on funding entrenches a subordinate relationship between VCOs and public authorities. In some case study sites, the focus on a wider 'compact' has allowed a more mature relationship to develop:

"It's given elected members a different experience of the voluntary sector – normally they see us when we are saying we don't have enough money and please don't close our project." (VCS respondent)

"Because it is not about money it is easier." (VCS respondent)

Investment in infrastructure is essential if the sector is to pursue its *diverse interests* effectively, both in compact development and in partnership more generally. The position of the BME VCS is particularly problematic and needs to be addressed both by local public bodies and by the mainstream VCS. At present, there is no doubt that BME organisations – in all areas, and despite, in some case study sites, the existence of effective and longstanding BME organisations – feel marginal to the process of compact development. Many BME organisations had not

heard of the national compact, some had not even heard of the local compact and only one had heard of the code of practice for BME organisations. Even those which had heard of the compact or had been involved in early discussions, felt ignored as it developed further.

This mirrored more general views from BME organisations: comments such as 'we always get left to deal with relatively junior officers' were made, and a common criticism made by BME organisations was that they did not get a fair share of resources for developing local infrastructure. It is clear that existing networks cannot effectively represent the interests of BME communities, even where they attempt or claim to do so. BME organisations often faced what they saw as a classic dilemma; barriers were placed in the way of their participation, and they were then accused of 'not being interested'. In one site, BME groups accused local authority officers of 'cherry-picking' BME groups and individuals, often not representative of the broader BME communities, to co-opt onto committees. All these concerns may well be expressed by organisations of disabled people, gay and lesbian organisations, or others representing excluded communities – we did not study these in depth.

Although BME organisations are critical of local authorities and mainstream VCS organisations, some short-term funding is now being made available to such groups independent of local authorities, for example through the Connecting Communities Programme sponsored by the Home Office. This aims to build local capacity for BME organisations but for them, as for other groups currently marginal to the compact and wider partnership process, the key medium-term question perhaps is how to ensure they can take an appropriately central part in mainstream partnership work rather than continue to be supported at the margins. This will depend significantly on infrastructure. There is a stipulation in the guidelines for the Community Empowerment Fund that this should be used to engage BME groups with the LSP process and, of course, there is funding for BME infrastructure at regional level. It remains to be seen how this potential will develop over time.

Finally, it was already clear from the initial mapping study that compacts would only work if there was a clear framework for *review*; this was built in in some but not all of our case study areas. If the compact is to be more than a piece of paper, it requires an action plan with clear indicators of success, of the kinds outlined earlier, and mechanisms for ongoing audit and review as well as sanctions where the principles are not adhered to. This in turn requires transparency and commitment from all agencies operating at local level – statutory, voluntary and community. Ultimately the compact has to be a dynamic rather than a static document, a reference point against which to assess the development of relationships between public authorities and the VCS and one which evolves as those relationships themselves change.

The future

Respondents pointed to a number of indicators by which they would assess progress in compact development. This tentative framework for evaluation is reproduced below.

Assessing progress

- Information and promotion:

- All VCOs knowing about the compact and about how they could use it.

- All local authority departments knowing there is a compact and what it is for – this to include information in all recruitment packs and induction processes.

- The appointment of officers with responsibilities for the VCS, and secondments between local public bodies and the VCS.

- Involvement of a range of organisations and not just the ones the local authority funds.

- Evidence of energy being put into finding out about how to engage with different interest groups.

- Other agencies wanting to join the compacts process; demand for involvement in the process from 'below'.

- Transfer of compact gains to other similar initiatives so that other partnerships work better; evidence that the compact is being referred to in other policy initiatives.

- Visible gains for the wider community.

This agenda has some way to go in most sites. So far, the experience of compact negotiation suggests that positive progress has been made, but there are key issues about time and resources, about how far awareness of the compact has penetrated into either sector and about the balance of power and trust between the parties concerned.

Earlier in this report, we put forward a number of different scenarios as a basis for assessing compacts. They could herald an equal partnership between sectors, with the VCS as 'senior partners' in the welfare firm. They could be used to incorporate the sector into a government agenda – the danger that Dahrendorf cautioned against in his 2001 Arnold Goodman lecture (Dahrendorf, 2001). They could be the thin end of the wedge for local government as central government pushes through a more devolved system of decision making and delivery. They could simply be a piece of paper which makes no difference to anything. What does our evidence say about the ways in which local developments mirror these scenarios?

Our evidence so far suggests that the 'senior partner' scenario has not yet been achieved. Local authorities are still seen to hold most of the cards by VCOs, although some of the latter are becoming more assertive and realising their increased power. The incorporation danger is perhaps belied by the fact that many local VCOs have been the initiators of the compact as a means of providing them with the space and conditions whereby they can function effectively and getting them on level terms with their proposed partners. Whether incorporation creeps up on them, however, remains to be seen – some BME organisations clearly fear that this may be an outcome of the compact. On the other hand, however, some people in local authorities definitely see the compact as the thin end of an unwelcome wedge (perhaps associating it with the local government modernisation agenda which is not equally welcome across all local authorities) and are distrustful of its advance. But there are positive examples where those involved see benefits for both sides and the commitment of the major national intermediary bodies is encouraging.

What most respondents were acutely aware of was that compacts were not in any way binding, they held no legal force and could be seen as a temporary and transitory phenomenon. But they were not just 'a piece of paper'. At their most unambitious, respondents saw compacts as providing a reference point against which to measure local authority and other public body practice and hold these bodies to account; more positively, they felt that compacts would help to develop the understanding between the sectors which is still patently lacking. Indeed the perseverance shown in some sites demonstrates the importance which the key players attach to it.

It is too early to say, however, how compacts will work out in practice or play out against other developments. As yet, the progress of compacts acts more as a reflection of the current state of relationships between the sectors than a pointer to the future. In that sense, the jury is still out. Much will depend on how the compacts are used in practice and the extent to which the principles are translated into concrete codes of practice – themselves also more than just 'a piece of paper' – which can then be enforced on both sides. But equally important will be the extent to which compacts can be used to push at the boundaries, to encourage innovative practice and to take relationships into new directions.

Perhaps the best indicator of progress will be when compacts cease to be seen as a way to boost the position of the VCS in an environment which they feel disadvantages them, on the one hand, or something which depends on local authority champions because most local authority staff still see it as an irrelevance, on the other. Success will have come when compacts are a negotiation between equals towards common goals, building on trust rather than compensating in a formal or contractual way for a lack of trust. This may address the paradox pointed to by Dahrendorf (2001) who observed in the compact both the requirement for government to recognise the independence of the voluntary sector but also the increasing dependence of that part he described as 'the compact sector which benefits from organised relations with government' on government funding.

The idea of a compact is about the shifting relationships between different sectors and agencies in a rapidly changing policy environment. As such it needs to be dynamic and respond to changes in the nature of local government and governance. If so, one particularly significant recent development is the introduction of LSPs which will bring local agencies together with VCOs to improve services and contribute to the development of community strategies. These bodies may well need to consider whether they should take over and broaden the compact and this will have implications not only for the relationship of different parts of government with the VCS, but also the relationships and understandings between the different parts of government themselves. There has also been some discussion of how the local business sector could fit into such an understanding; and there needs to be much more thought about how the compact idea informs regional governance arrangements.

As partnership forms of working extend, a clearer understanding of the different contributions each partner can make and how they can best support and complement each other will become increasingly essential. The 'compact' idea and particularly the process of mutual understanding it involves could be a valuable precedent and driving force, as a framework for more extensive agreements and as a template for partnership working in general. As one of our participants put it, the principles of the compact should become a 'way of life' and be transferred to other relationships and initiatives. This seems a rather grand agenda for a piece of paper, but research study after research study suggests that partnerships founder on the lack of clarity at the outset, misunderstanding and even lack of respect between partners, inequities of resources, and imbalances of power. Without some kind of framework and the institutional learning it represents, progress in partnership will continue to be piecemeal and rushed, to reinvent wheels (often square rather than round), and to reproduce these imbalances of power.

However, it is also important to consider whether there will come a time when, as one respondent in our research put it, "we need to let go of the word 'compact' and move on". In an increasingly complex welfare mix, and as the boundaries between sectors blur and shift, perhaps our understanding of the agreements and principles that will need to govern relationships will itself need to become more sophisticated and the notion of written agreements as the basis for trust may seem a bit primitive. Ironically, the success of compacts may be best judged when they become redundant as the lessons learnt from their construction are identified and applied to new partnership working. A compact might be as good as any place to start to address the kinds of issues raised earlier, and to develop the confidence on which more trusting relationships can be based (Fenton et al, 1999). It is likely to continue to be needed unless partnership cultures change. But as the issues begin to be resolved, so the reality of the compact itself might fade from the scene.

References

Balloch, S. and Taylor, M. (eds) (2001)
Partnership working: Policy and practice, Bristol:
The Policy Press.

Bloor, K. (1999) *Comparing national compacts*,
Working Paper No 2, Brighton/Hull: University
of Brighton/University of Hull.

Clarke, M. and Stewart, J. (1997) *Partnership and
the management of cooperation*, Birmingham:
INLOGOV.

Colenutt, B. and Cullen, A. (1994) 'Community
empowerment in vogue or vain?', *Local
Economy*, vol 9, no 3, pp 236-50.

Craig, G. and Manthorpe, J. (1999) 'Unequal
partners?', *Social Policy and Administration*, vol
33, no 1, March, pp 55-72.

Craig, G. and Taylor, M. (2000) *Local government
and the third sector: Papering over the cracks*,
Working Paper No 3, Brighton/Hull: University
of Brighton/University of Hull.

Craig, G.,Taylor, M., Szanto, C. and Wilkinson, M.,
(1999) *Developing local compacts*, York: York
Publishing Services.

Craig, G., Warburton, D., Monro, S., Taylor, M.
and Wilkinson, M. (2001) 'Willing partners?
Voluntary and community associations and local
democracy', Paper to Social Policy Association
conference, Belfast, 24-26 July.

Dahrendorf, R. (2001) 'Challenges to the voluntary
sector', Arnold Goodman Lecture, Charities Aid
Foundation, July.

Deakin, N. (1995) *Commission on the future of the
voluntary sector*, London: National Council of
Voluntary Organisations.

DTLR (Department for Transport, Local
Government and the Regions) (2001) 'The
Community Empowerment Fund' at
www.neighbourhood.dtlr.gov.uk/empfund

Fenton, N., Hems, L. and Passey, A. (1999) 'Trust,
the voluntary sector and civil society',
*International Journal of Sociology and Social
Policy*, vol 19, no 7/8, pp 21-42.

Ferlie, E., Ashburner, L., Fitzgerald, L. and
Pettigrew, A. (1997) *The new public
management in action*, Oxford: Oxford
University Press.

Gaster, L., Deakin, N., Riseborough, M., McCabe,
A., Wainwright, S. and Rogers, S. (1999) *History,
strategy or lottery?* London: Improvement and
Development Agency.

Hems, L. and Passey, A. (1998) *The voluntary
sector almanac*, London: National Council of
Voluntary Organisations.

Home Office (1998) *Getting it right together:
Compact on relations between government and
the voluntary and community sector in England*,
Cm 4100, London: The Stationery Office.

Humberside TEC (2000) *Valuing the voluntary
sector in Humberside*, Hull: Humberside TEC.

Hunter, M. (1999) 'A third way for charities?',
Community Care, 7 January, pp 18-19.

JRF (Joseph Rowntree Foundation) (2001) *Evaluating the significance of local compacts*, JRF Findings No 251, February.

Labour Party (1997) *Building the future together: Labour's policies for partnership between government and the voluntary sector*, London: Labour Party.

LGA (Local Government Association) (2000) *Compacts, strategies, partnerships*, London: LGA.

McCurry, P. (2001) 'Putting down new roots', *Community Care*, 30 August-5 September, pp 18-19.

NYFVO (North Yorkshire Forum for Voluntary Organisations) (2000) *Valuing the voluntary and community sector in North Yorkshire and York*, Thirsk: NYFVO.

Owen, D. (1964) *English philanthropy 1660-1960*, London: Oxford University Press.

Policy & Politics (2001) Special issue on Best Value, vol 29, no 4, Bristol.

Powell, M., Glendinning, C. and Rummery, K. (eds) (2002) *Partnerships, New Labour and the governance of welfare*, Bristol: The Policy Press.

SCVO (Scottish Council for Voluntary Organisations) (1997a) *Head and heart*, Kemp report, Edinburgh: SCVO.

SCVO (Scottish Council for Voluntary Organisations) (1997b) 'Scottish councils' voluntary sector policy statements', Edinburgh: SCVO, mimeo.

SCVO/CoSLA (Scottish Council for Voluntary Organisations/Convention of Scottish Local Authorities) (1995) *Positive partnership*, Edinburgh: SCVO/CoSLA.

SEU (Social Exclusion Unit) (1998) *Bringing Britain together: A national strategy for neighbourhood renewal*, London: The Stationery Office.

SEU (Social Exclusion Unit) (2001) *A new commitment to neighbourhood regeneration: The action plan*, London: The Stationery Office.

Sykes, R. and Clinton, C. (2000) *Compact with the community*, LGA Research Report No 5, London: LGA.

Walkley, N. (2001) *Best value: Streamlining*, Discussion Paper No 1, London: Improvement and Development Agency.

WGGRS/LGA (Working Group on Government Relations Secretariat/Local Government Association) (2000) *Local compact guidelines: Getting local relationships right together*, London: WGGRS/LGA.

Wilkinson, M. (1999) *Key themes and areas of consideration for best practice*, Working Paper No 1, Brighton/Hull: University of Brighton/University of Hull.

WLGA/WCVA (Welsh Local Government Assocation/Wales Council for Voluntary Action) (1997) *Achieving shared aims: Working to a common agenda between local authorities and the voluntary sector*, Cardiff: WLGA/WCVA.

Wolfenden, Lord (1978) *The future of voluntary organisations*, London: Croom Helm.

Appendix A: The research

In 1999, the research team responsible for this report published the findings of a preliminary study which mapped the development of local agreements and policies about the relationship between local public sector bodies and the VCS (Craig et al, 1999; see also JRF, 2001). That preliminary study took place prior to the launch of the national compacts late in 1998. Its main conclusions were that:

- The development of a national framework (the national compacts) was a valuable asset in the development of local policies and agreements but should not be used as a prototype.
- Most successful policies and agreements were emerging in areas where there was a positive history of dialogue between the VCS and the local authority.
- The successful development of a policy or agreement required a well-supported VCS infrastructure that could reflect the views of different parts of the VCS, including smaller unfunded organisations and the BME VCS.
- The process of developing a policy or agreement was as important as the policy itself.
- The success of a policy or agreement depended on having an ongoing structure for dialogue and review.

Other important findings from that mapping study included the need for an appreciation of the historical development of the local VCS (a point which shaped our choice of case study sites in the follow-up study – see below); the importance of having champions – 'the right person in the right place at the right time' – to follow through developments; the need for adequate human and financial resources to support compact development; and the importance of

understanding compacts as being much more than simply to do with the funding of the VCS.

The mapping report was followed by a series of working papers which explored a range of detailed issues arising from that study, including issues of best practice (Wilkinson, 1999), the difference between the development of national compacts in England, Scotland and Wales (Bloor, 1999) and the place of compacts within the broader development of partnership working within local government in England (Craig and Taylor, 2000).

Following on from the mapping study, the JRF agreed to fund a detailed study evaluating the development of local compacts in a number of case study sites. This follow-on study ran from early 1999 to mid-2001. Late in 2000, the Foundation also provided supplementary funding to explore the specific position and perspectives of BME VCOs towards the development of local compacts. The need for this had become clear to the research team during the course of the main follow-on study, which had pointed to a general lack of engagement between BME organisations and the process of local compact development. The BME 'extension' study ran for six months from January 2001, in parallel with the final stages of the main study and was carried out by Alia Syed, in liaison with the main research team. This report incorporates the findings from both the main follow-on study and the BME extension.

In the main study, 10 case study sites were chosen and were each visited or contacted on three separate occasions by a member of the research team in order to collect documentary material and to interview a range of key respondents from local government, the VCS and other local public bodies where appropriate (particularly health authorities/boards [in Scotland] and trusts, police authorities and TECs [and their Scottish equivalents, Local Enterprise Companies]). The case study sites were chosen to reflect a range of local contexts, in terms particularly of type of authority, local demography – ensuring several areas with a relatively large BME population were selected – and local political traditions. In our view, local political tradition could be seen as a proxy for thinking about the way in which local VCS had developed in terms of size, funding and opportunities for engagement with statutory bodies. The case study sites were located across England (six sites), Scotland (two sites) and Wales (two sites). In addition we gathered some information on two further English sites, with which we had substantial contact during the course of the study as a result of other work with which the research team was engaged. The team also had access to policy papers from and ongoing discussion with national organisations representing either local government (the Local Government Association, the Welsh Local Government Association and the Convention of Scottish Local Authorities), the VCS (particularly the National Council for Voluntary Organisations, the National Association of Councils for Voluntary Service, the Urban Forum, Action for Communities in Rural England and Community Sector Coalition), and other representative bodies at national level.

For the BME extension study, data was collected in four of our 10 initial case study sites: the three urban areas with the greatest proportionate BME population and a deeply rural area with a relatively small BME population. In these areas, the researcher – an experienced researcher of South Asian origin – made contact solely with BME organisations (including some not identified in the main study), accessing them independently of the main LDAs in the locality. Just over 20 such organisations were interviewed. This report also incorporates data from BME organisations contacted by the researchers in the main study. Many organisations contacted through the main study also claimed to represent both white and BME constituencies although, in the judgement of the researchers, the validity of these claims varied quite markedly. The team wishes to acknowledge, with thanks, the help of all those who contributed to this study.

The 10 case study sites and the two supplementary sites are anonymised here to protect the identity of respondents. They included unitary authorities (two each in Wales and Scotland – where all local authorities are unitary following local government reorganisation in 1996 – and two in England, of very different kinds, following English local government reorganisation between 1995 and 1998), two metropolitan boroughs, one London borough and one shire county covering a two-tier local government area. Case study sites were also chosen to include areas where local compact development was either well-advanced or barely underway, one where no overall local VCS development agency was in existence, and one where local health organisations were strongly involved in local compact development. Despite our best attempts, it proved impossible to find a suitable case study site where a TEC or LEC had had a significant input into the compact process, although one of our sites subsequently developed a compact with the local TEC. The case study sites also included two deeply rural areas, several mixed urban/rural areas and several inner city urban areas. Although some of the early thinking about compacts was reflected in discussions within the VCS in Northern Ireland, the markedly different local government arrangements there meant that we did not feel it appropriate to extend this study to the province.

On average, about 40 interviews (including second and third interviews, and face-to-face and telephone interviews) were conducted in each of the case study sites for the main study, using topic guides developed specifically for this study. The two supplementary sites were both unitary authorities, one with no local VCS development agency.

Appendix B: The case study sites

Site 1

The 'compact' process in this Labour controlled city began prior to local government reorganisation in 1996 with a conference between the transitional council and the VCS. There was already a strong history of VCS and tenant involvement in local authority affairs. Within the VCS, there are a series of forums within the sector presenting different interests within the VCS, but in the past the relationship with the local authority has been dominated by social care. A driving factor for the partnership agreement was the need to take an agreed approach to funding cuts. A partnership agreement was drawn up by a cross-sector working group and endorsed by the local authority in late November of that year. Later, in 1997, a monitoring development group was set up to develop an implementation plan and oversee developments, but its terms of reference were unclear, the commitment of different council departments was variable and it became a 'talking shop'.

After another two years, in 1999, the key players on both sides proposed two subgroups to look at service delivery and governance issues, but these did not work either. It is lead officers from both sectors who have driven the process forward. Part of the problem in developing and monitoring the agreement has been the lack of time on both sides. But in late 2000, core funding to the LDA from the Scottish Executive provided a 'massive boost'. In July 2001 a joint working group was formed to turn the partnership statement into a compact and to provide formal mechanisms for monitoring the relationship. The increasing importance of the Community Planning agenda seems to have breathed new life into the process. Participants feel that they have been through the 'forming' and 'storming' stage and are now at the 'norming' stage.

Site 2

The development of the compact in this area was a policy imperative for the local authority in response to imminent local government reorganisation in 1996. The importance of developing and fostering good relationships with the voluntary sector was also highlighted by the large-scale spending cuts that accompanied the reorganisation process. The compact was taken forward jointly by the local authority and the VCS. It was championed by senior managers in the local authority and a new VCS LDA, established in 1997, carried forward the strong commitment in that sector to the development of a compact.

There seems to be general agreement that the VCS has grown considerably since reorganisation and is now very diverse and dynamic. The LDA has 12 interest-based forums which elect representatives onto joint planning groups and there is a wider Voluntary Sector Forum (VSF) to ensure that these mechanisms do not exclude other views.

The compact was launched in 1997. It has not only a set of broad statements but also a set of clear implementable objectives. The key officers report back to a liaison committee which aims to meet twice a year. This schedule has slipped and as a result relationships between the participants are still a bit formal – people are not yet familiar with each other. Key players from both sectors have heavy workloads and this has prevented concerted effort to improve this formal liaison. However, informal joint working has mushroomed and professional relationships at corporate departmental and individual levels are said to be flourishing.

The compact has been reviewed and is felt to be robust enough to continue as it is. Similar compacts have meanwhile been negotiated with the health authority and NHS trusts, and a four-way compact is about to be launched.

Site 3

The local authority in this site was one of the unitaries created by local government reorganisation. The local compact was a VCS initiative which began in 1998. It was developed within the VCS before being presented to the local authority in autumn 2000. The wider VCS has been involved through twice-yearly consultation events, the first in autumn 1998.

Our research suggests that the process of integration within the local authority was slow. There is no locality-wide VCS infrastructure. There are, however, five fairly small VCS LDAs, which used to relate to district councils and are based in different parts of the locality. Their make-up varies considerably and there are some overlaps in role between the different bodies, but they come together through an unfunded Development Agencies Network. This feeds into the local authority through delegated subgroups. The population is quite dispersed which creates problems for representation and communication within the sector.

There are two sets of local area fora, developed by the health authority and by the county council as mechanisms for better communications and consultation with the VCS. The centre for partnership work in the public sector is a high profile Pathfinder Initiative which has brought together all the major local players, including the VCS, which is represented on the board, the management group and which chairs a number of its working groups.

As a result of these different factors, relationships between the sectors are quite complex and can be fragmented, while some VSOs whose coverage is not area-based may not be served by a locality-based infrastructure. Funding for the infrastructure is quite low and relationships between the sector and the local authority are said to be largely contract-based.

The compact has been through two drafts and is not yet at a final stage. The failure to involve the local authority at an early stage is now seen to be a problem and the lack of progress meant that the initiative lost momentum. However, this has changed recently and there is now more optimism. The most recent draft relates some of the key compact themes much more closely to the pathfinder partnership structures and has the potential to bring a range of players on board.

Site 4

In this site – a unitary authority covering six towns – the national compact provided an opportunity to put a framework around cross-sector relationships that some key players felt were already happening, especially in the social care and regeneration fields. Within the last six years, a new VCS LDA was formed. More recently, a review of local authority relationships with the voluntary sector was commissioned. This review, which reported in 1999, reflected the need to bring greater transparency and openness to the relationships between members, officers and the VCS, particularly local authority funded groups. A set of documents was produced to clarify roles and relationships.

While the review was in progress, a compact implementation group was set up and a compact was launched in November 1999, based on the national compact. The compact included a compact implementation plan. As a result, work is being done to replace grants with service level agreements and a number of other jointly agreed procedures have been produced. The LDA produces an information newsletter that regularly updates the VCS on the progress of the implementation of the compact action plan.

A VSF is being developed to involve VCOs more directly in further development of the compact and in structures and mechanisms for policy consultation. A recent review of the compact raised issues about how far the compact reflected the diversity of the sector – and particularly the needs of smaller and unfunded groups. It also raised issues about equal opportunities within the VCS, about protocols for grants and about feedback mechanisms. Clarification of member and officer roles and the introduction of service level agreements were seen as positive developments.

There is also a civic partnership in the locality which gives the VCS access, through the LDA and the Racial Equality Council, to the major public sector bodies. New town committees and forums are being set up for each town. In April 2000 the local authority restructured around corporate themes. There is a community involvement steering group as part of the health partnership in the locality.

Site 5

The local authority in this site, which covers a large geographical area, became a unitary authority in 1996 and this was followed by a further complex restructuring within the authority. The modernisation agenda has added a further layer of reform with the adoption of a Cabinet system. The council had in the past set up a number of initiatives to audit support for the voluntary sector and also developed a community development strategy, but no moves had been made towards a compact. Relationships between the two sectors were mixed and variable across the county.

Following the directive from the Welsh First Secretary, the LDA (which had been set up post reorganisation) set up public meetings with VCOs in the locality. In late 1999 a compact working group was set up involving the local authority and the VCS. A joint statement was issued in early 2000 but little further progress was made.

Local elections in May 2000 led to a change of leadership in the local authority, although Labour stayed in power. The VCS, through the LDA, was drawn more closely into council processes with presentations to the Social Inclusion Forum and the Best Value Link Officers' Group. In late 2000 a second draft of the compact was agreed to be sent out for consultation. Things have moved on since then, with higher level commitment from the local Authority and the compact was launched in June 2001. A community liaison group is being set up to oversee its implementation. There is a separate compact with the health authority and one is about to be signed with the Learning and Skills Council.

Site 6

The VCS in this London borough is large and very diverse, including a sizeable BME sector. Local compact developments were started in early 1999, in response to the national compact. A draft compact was produced and given a high profile launch, but a local byelection at the end of the year swung the local council from Labour to Liberal Democrat and the whole process floundered. Cuts which had been planned by Labour were enforced fairly drastically by the new Liberal Democrat administration and a large number of groups, especially in the BME sector, were hit hard (with an 80% cut over the years). This led to a total breakdown in communications. The funding that remained was increasingly contract-based, with the VCS seen largely in the role of service deliverers. The new local administration also commissioned a review of the voluntary sector, which was quite heavily criticised by the sector.

Several factors have improved the situation since that time. First, by autumn 2000 communications had been restored between the council and the VCS intermediary body and the council agreed to fund a partnership officer for the intermediary body. Second, while there had been a history of tension between the intermediary body and VCS organisations, these relationships have improved. Third, there is a sense in which the conflict has made the local VCS less dependent on the council and more assertive, although the BME VCS and other smaller organisations are still struggling. There is a need for BME organisations to have their own infrastructure resources. But the fourth, and some feel the most significant factor, is the LSP initiative and the arrival of the Community Empowerment Fund, along with the involvement of government's regional office. These latest developments have the potential to make a real difference, support the voluntary sector infrastructure and bring the local authority to the negotiating table.

Site 7

The initiative for developing a partnership agreement in this locality came from the local authority. Following reorganisation, it supported the formation of a LDA, and in early 1998 produced a draft partnership statement, which was very much based on a perception of the VCS as a service provider. Until January 2001, the process of agreeing the statement was held up by the need for the LDA to obtain secure funding and premises and train up its management committee. But in 2000 the council set up a unilateral review of relationships with the VCS, again based firmly in a commissioning agenda. However, core funding from the Scottish Executive to the LDA provided a massive boost to the VCS. At the same time the LDA received funding to develop a separate compact for the local Social Inclusion Partnership.

The locality covers two quite distinct areas and it is difficult to pull together a coherent VCS view. There is also a BME sector forum, but it has not been effective. It is also difficult to bring together a coordinated approach in a local authority where relationships with the sector are dominated by social work. However, the new resources going into the VCS infrastructure and a commitment from the council's Head of Community Resources at a relaunch in February 2001 to develop a new council-wide compact suggest that the future is looking more rosy.

Site 8

This site is another of the new unitary councils formed in 1996. The compact process in this site began before local government reorganisation in 1995 when the chief executive in the VCS intermediary agency contacted the county council to promote the idea of a joint partnership statement. A joint working group was formed, but the process stalled when the chief executive of the intermediary body left and was not replaced for a year or so. A VSF was, however, formed with the support of the chief executive and recent relationships between the sectors have been largely positive. The arrival of a new chief executive for the intermediary body in 1998 put the compact back on the agenda, and six months later a community support officer was seconded by the council to the VCS intermediary body to develop the compact.

After a consultation event in late 1999, a new joint steering group involving members, officers and VSF representatives was formed to drive the compact forward to a launch in late 2000. But imminent council restructuring first delayed and then stalled the process. The disbanding of the council's Policy Unit meant the community support officer post disappeared. However, the arrival in 2001 of LSPs and the Community Empowerment Fund was seen by the VCS to have given the whole process a boost, with the potential for Community Empowerment Funding development monies to support the compact process locally: it has 'changed the complexion totally' and would 'make a huge difference locally'. This case study underlines the importance of key players in keeping the process going.

Site 9

The county VSF contacted the health authority in this locality in 1998 to develop a compact and a working group was established in 1999. The initiative was driven by NHS reorganisation and the need for a framework to maintain what were generally seen as positive relations. A draft compact went out for consultation in early 2000 and a conference was held later in the year. A final draft was agreed in January 2001. All the LDAs in the county and all but two key health bodies had signed up at the time of this report.

The compact was closely modelled on a parallel compact signed between the local authority and the VCS in the main city in the region – the director of the LDA there had been involved in this county-wide initiative. February 2001 saw the first code of practice completed and a second one is imminent. There are concerns that continuing reorganisation within the NHS will slow down the implementation and hence impact of the compact. All parties feel that it will provide a solid framework for relationships once reorganisation beds in – in about two years' time.

Site 10

The compact negotiations in this site began in 1999, following a contact between the council and the VCS intermediary body. The government regional office was also drawn into the process and in the spring of 2000 a steering group was formed in the VCS. The two sectors then presented the idea of a compact to the NHS Joint Commissioning Forum and an existing LSP, who both agreed in principle to come on board. A conference late in 2000 drew together a new steering group across the sectors. However, a failure to agree on funding for the post of a compact development officer meant that this post never materialised and little progress was made. The arrival of LSPs and the Community Empowerment Fund, however, has the potential to revitalise the process, within the framework of the LSP and with resources for a community development officer to progress the compact. People now feel 'the prospects are all pretty positive'.

Site 11

This site is another unitary authority created in local government reorganisation in a metropolitan area, which used to be covered by the county council and district councils. The VCS intermediary bodies in the two main districts were merged alongside local government reorganisation, but the new unified body closed down in 1999. A VSF, with limited staffing, is now the main channel for VCS representation.

The compact was the initiative of the VSF, which saw it as an opportunity to create an improved framework for relationships not only with the local authority and the VCS but also with other public bodies. A draft was drawn up by a working group and considered by a well-attended meeting of the VSF in December 1999 where amendments were suggested. Elections were held in the spring of 2000 to form a cross-sector group, which was set up and serviced by the VSF, to ensure a monthly meeting between the VCS and the council.

Once a revised draft had been agreed in the summer of 2000, this was presented to the local authority and other public bodies and a response requested within five months to allow for a launch in Spring 2001. With public sector negotiations led by officers from the local authority and the primary care group, this timetable was achieved and the launch duly went ahead with the signatories including the local authority, the health authority, the primary care group, the fire service, the police, the government regional office, the local New Deal for Communities, and the regional development agency. Codes of practice are now being drawn up. Three have been through the consultation process: information and communications, consultation and funding. Three more are planned on partnership working, representation and monitoring and evaluation.

The compact and the codes are progressed through the regular quarterly meetings of the VSF and the monthly dialogue meetings between representatives from the VSF and the public sector.

Site 12

This site is a medium-sized unitary authority created in 1996 by separation from a surrounding county council. The local CVS and local authority began joint work in early 1999 on the production of a compact document following the publication of the English national compact late in 1998. Initially the local compact document made extensive use of the national document and progress was quite speedy: by the summer of 1999, a draft compact was discussed and work began on five codes of practice (funding, consultation and policy development, the use of volunteers, monitoring and evaluation of local services, and BME groups). At the same time, work was undertaken to coordinate discussions between the local partners and those in the neighbouring county where a compact involving health service organisations (covering the unitary authority) was being developed.

By late 1999, when the draft compact had been submitted by the local working group formally to the local authority and the VCS, it appeared that work in this site had moved ahead of the national working party to develop guidelines for local compacts and some of the local experience was fed to the national level to inform their thinking. At the same time, it was recognised locally that compact thinking might be lost as national thinking on community planning (later LSPs) began to emerge and a deliberate attempt was made to link the compact to the emerging community planning process. Work on developing the local codes of practice was, however, slow because of other pressures on the local VCS, but drafts were produced by summer 2000 of four codes (all bar the code on monitoring and evaluation), by which time the local authority had formally adopted the compact itself. Later in 2000, a joint group with representatives from the local authority, local NHS organisations and the VCS was established to oversee the review process and encourage further development of the compact. Although the importance of process was acknowledged locally, and it was felt that the work on the compact BME code may have had an impact in confirming the need for special funding for local BME groups, the local VCS felt that the agreement of the local compact had been unduly prolonged. Despite some local tensions, its production has been relatively unproblematic and it remains to be seen how effective it may be in managing major difficulties locally.